The Strategic Defense Initiative

SUNY Series in the Making of Foreign Policy:
Theories and Issues
ALEX R. HYBEL, editor

The Strategic Defense Initiative

Symbolic Containment of the Nuclear Threat

REBECCA S. BJORK

State University of New York Press

The author is grateful to the American Humanist Association for permission
to reprint portions of "A Commitment to Life," by Helen Caldicott, which first
appeared in the September/October 1982 issue of *The Humanist.*

Published by
State University of New York Press, Albany

For information, address State University of New York
Press, State University Plaza, Albany, NY 12246

Production by Bernadine Dawes
Marketing by Lynne Lekakis

Library of Congress Cataloging-in-Publication Data

Bjork, Rebecca, 1961–
      The strategic defense initiative / symbolic containment of the
nuclear threat / Rebecca S. Bjork.
            p.   cm. — (SUNY series in the making of foreign policy)
      Includes bibliographical references (p.   ) and index.
      ISBN 0–7914–1161–3 (HC : acid-free paper) : $44.50. — ISBN
0–7914–1162–1 (PB : acid-free paper) : $14.95
            1. Rhetoric—Political aspects—United States. 2. Strategic
Defense Initiative. 3. Reagan, Ronald—Oratory. 4. Bush, George,
1924– —Oratory. 5. Communication in politics—United States.
I. Title. II. Series.
PN239.P64B56   1992
808.83—dc20
91–34487
CIP

10 9 8 7 6 5 4 3 2 1

For Kristin, Angela, Nathan,
Allison, and LeAnn
and your future

Contents

Preface ix

Chapter 1
Toward a Rhetorical Understanding of SDI 1

Chapter 2
Innocence and Destiny in American Foreign Policy 21

Chapter 3
Rhetorical Challenges to the Arms Race 41

Chapter 4
The Symbolic Power of SDI 65

Chapter 5
The "New World Order" and SDI 91

Chapter 6
Public Debate in an Age of Strategic Defense 115

Notes 133

Works Cited 161

Index 177

Preface

AS AN AVID OBSERVER of world politics and particularly, nuclear weapons issues, I was both surprised and fascinated when President Ronald Reagan proposed the Strategic Defense Initiative in a nationally televised speech in 1983. The initiation of such a revolutionary weapon system at a time when U. S.–Soviet relations were at a low point, and public activism against the nuclear arms race reached a pinnacle, seemed to mark an important defining moment for Reagan's nuclear policies. The SDI proposal set in motion an enduring national and international controversy, as administration officials and critics alike discussed the merits and drawbacks of the program in public forums.

As a graduate student in the Department of Communication Arts and Sciences at the University of Southern California, I was interested in the ways in which foreign policy is constructed through language, and SDI seemed to be an interesting case study through which to explore the symbolic nature of U. S. nuclear weapons policies. This analysis of the discursive constructions of the SDI program during the Reagan and Bush administrations emerged as the culmination of these interests.

My guiding assumption in this work is that "reality" is discursively constructed, in that human beings use language to define situations, interpret events, and respond creatively to material conditions. Viewing international relations from this perspective calls into question the notion that foreign policy exists in some extra-discursive realm, that it has existence beyond the language and symbols used to describe it. Given this assumption, foreign policy, including SDI, can be "read" as text and analyzed in terms of its symbolic, discursive implications. Focusing on the symbolic nature of foreign policy leads to some important conclusions regarding the role of the Strategic Defense Initiative in global affairs, and the implications of pursuing critical analyses of foreign policy discourse.

Since this book went into production, many dramatic changes have taken place in the world arena. The dissolution of the Soviet Union, Mikhail Gorbachev's fall from power, the formation of the Commonwealth of Independent States, and the emerging tensions between the Russian Federation and Ukraine, for example, illustrate the unpredictable nature of international relations in the post-Cold War world. The bulk of this book was written before the onset of these upheavals; hence, references to Gorbachev and "the Soviet Union" that appear throughout the text should be understood in historical terms. The arguments made in chapter 5 concerning the role of SDI at the end of the Cold War seem especially relevant at this writing, in that the solidification of U.S. global leadership, especially in the United Nations, is evident in such events as the imposition of sanctions against Libya for its role in promoting acts of international terrorism. As is always the case, the passage of time will alter our understanding of world affairs. I can only hope that this book will make a contribution to the growing body of literature concerning what is rapidly becoming a product of historical understanding; the Cold War.

Students of rhetoric, political communication, international relations, political science, and strategic studies hopefully will find this book to be an important contribution to the existing literature on SDI, U. S. foreign policy, and rhetorical criticism and theory. It is perhaps most appropriate for advanced undergraduate and graduate courses in these fields.

There are many people who deserve public thanks for their help with this project. Alex R. Hybel, Clay Morgan, and the staff of the State University of New York Press were most helpful in the preparation of this manuscript. The reviewers provided insightful and important contributions to my work, and I am indebted to them for their time and efforts. My instructors at the University of Southern California, Thomas A. Hollihan, Alex R. Hybel, Randall A. Lake, and Walter R. Fisher, to name only a few, were dedicated and demanding teachers who inspired and challenged me every step of the way. Many of my colleagues, including Malcolm O. Sillars, G. Thomas Goodnight, Janice Hocker Rushing, Dolores V. Tanno,

Carrie Crenshaw, Cori Dauber, and Reginald Twigg, spent long hours helping me formulate ideas, and provided professional and personal support. I am indebted to them all. Finally, my family, and especially my mother, Harriet L. Bjork, deserves the lions share of the credit for this work. Without their support, inspiration, and love, the world would be a much darker place.

1.
Toward a Rhetorical
Understanding of SDI

THE DETONATION OF THE FIRST ATOMIC BOMB in July, 1945 not only shook the New Mexico desert, but also shattered humanity's symbolic construction of the meaning of war. Before the onset of the atomic age, the ability to wreak devastation upon an enemy was stunning. But the destruction at Hiroshima and Nagasaki was a grisly signal to the world that, suddenly, everything was different. The basic power of the universe was harnessed in weaponry, and no defense seemed possible.

When human beings are confronted with a situation in which the ability to make sense of the world is outstripped by the complexities of the changing environment, they attempt to rectify the situation through the use of language or symbolic action.[1] Through language, humans redefine, reinterpret, and rename their situation, and attempt to establish order by creating meanings that make sense of events. Many such attempts at making sense of the nuclear age through language and other symbolic acts have been evident since 1945. But perhaps none are as controversial or compelling as the Strategic Defense Initiative (SDI).

In a televised address to the nation on March 23, 1983, President Ronald Reagan dramatically altered the national debate on nuclear weapons strategy and policy by proposing the Strategic Defense Initiative. Near the end of his address Reagan stated, "Let me share with you a vision of the future which offers hope. It is that we embark on a program to counter the awesome Soviet missile threat with measures that are defensive."[2] With these words, Reagan proposed a first step away from mutual assured destruction, toward a concept of mutual assured survival, marking "a major shift in the politics of the nuclear age."[3]

1

Most analyses of SDI are concerned with explaining either the technical controversies surrounding the program, or its effects on issues such as arms control, U. S.–Soviet relations, strategic policy, relationships with allies, and strategic stability.[4] While these studies are important, and contribute to a sophisticated understanding of the effects of SDI on international stability, they ignore a vital aspect of the program, one that can lead to important conclusions about SDI and about foreign policy in general. This neglected dimension is the symbolic or rhetorical power of SDI.

The Strategic Defense Initiative is not merely a collection of technical tools, research bodies, and bureaucratic organizations. Rather, it is an amalgamation of *meanings*; meanings which are shaped by and, in turn, shape a variety of linguistic, political, ideological, cultural, and social forces. These meanings create an understanding of SDI that becomes reality, in the sense that the symbolic understandings of the program influence policy and shape bureaucratic action, which themselves are symbolically constructed. The study of rhetoric, as the analysis and interpretation of public discourse that aims to reveal its various underlying symbolic appeals, is an appropriate way to explore these meanings associated with SDI and to explain their connection to the broader political and socio-cultural context. This approach is similar to the recent turn toward post-structuralist critiques of international relations, in that the focus of the analysis is on discourse.[5] Treating the "reality" of world politics as text underscores the increasing concern with modernist assumptions of objectivity, dualism, and rationality, and reflects an attempt to uncover relations of power as they are constructed and reified through language. Viewing SDI as a symbolic, rhetorical response to a difficult moral, political, military, and economic problem (the nuclear arms race) sheds light on SDI itself as well as the role that language plays in the formulation of American foreign policy.

In this study, I argue that SDI is a rhetorically powerful and appealing proposal to free Americans from the dilemmas of the nuclear arms race and fears about nuclear proliferation. To establish the nature of SDI's symbolic appeal, I propose to answer the following questions: (1) How did various actors in the Reagan and Bush Administrations justify SDI to public audiences? In other words, what rhetorical strategies were used to "sell" the program? (2) What roles do symbolic constructions of history and technology play in explaining the appeal of SDI? (3) How does understanding the symbolic aspects of SDI contribute to current discussions about the program itself, and the rhetoric of war and American foreign policy? (4) How does the prospect of strategic defense affect the functioning of public debate over nuclear weapons policy?

The Rhetorical Importance of SDI

Approaching the controversy over the Strategic Defense Initiative from a rhetorical perspective is appropriate for several reasons. First, as phenomena for study, nuclear war and its prevention are almost entirely textual. In other words, since a nuclear exchange has never occurred in the "real" world, all of humanity's experience with such an event is symbolic. As Jacques Derrida argues, "the phenomenon [of nuclear war] is fabulously textual also to the extent that, for the moment, a nuclear war has not taken place: one can only talk and write about it."[6] Since there has been no direct physical experience of all-out nuclear war, discussions of what it would be like, how military leaders would respond, how world leaders would behave, and how it could be prevented, are all grounded solely in discourse. Even scientific studies of the effects of nuclear war call upon severely limited empirical data from the Japanese experience and nuclear weapons tests.[7] Given this lack of direct physical experience with nuclear war, Derrida argues:

> [Nuclear war] has existence only through what is said of it, only where it is talked about. Some might call it a fable, then, a pure invention: in the sense in which it is said that a myth, an image, a fiction, a utopia, a rhetorical figure, a fantasy, a phantasm, are inventions.[8]

Since the rhetoric literally is the reality of nuclear war, the subject is well-suited to textual analysis. Nuclear weapons themselves can be "read" as text, as Timothy W. Luke's analysis of deterrence illustrates. He argues that the objective forms of nuclear weapons represent an exchange of meanings.[9] Viewing a weapon system like SDI as text allows the critic to explain the relationships between the weapon and the symbolic milieu from which it emerges and which it in turn helps to shape. Examining the discourse that justifies SDI allows the critic to explore the ways in which advocates call upon the symbolic artifacts of the culture to perpetuate the program, and shape the symbolic environment itself.

As Kenneth Burke argues, humans are "the symbol-using (symbol-making, symbol-misusing) animal[s]" who mold and shape their sense of reality through the use of language.[10] Human beings use symbols, but symbols also use us, in that the language chosen to describe our environment determines in large part how we behave in that environment. Hugh Dalziel Duncan claims, for example, that the "name" given to poverty shapes how society approaches solutions to poverty. If the impoverished are "lazy," they are treated with spite; if "victims," with compassion.[11] Similarly, the language used in naming nuclear weapons policies constitutes our sense of the "reality" of nuclear war, and, in this way, has the power to shape our actions—and our fate.

The role that nuclear weapons play in society is highly symbolic as well. Not only does language help to drive, justify, and perpetuate the continuation of the arms race, but nuclear weapons themselves are symbolically important. Ira Chernus argues that nuclear arms have taken on the symbolic meanings traditionally associated with religion. As omnipresent, all-powerful, apocalyptic devices that derive their power from the basic energy of the universe itself, nuclear weapons have taken on the symbolic trappings of a deity. Chernus observes that religious symbols of the deity:

> mediate a reality that seems to be infinite—unlimited in power, in knowledge, in space, and in time. This reality transcends rational comprehension; it seems to be alien, inscrutable, and unpredictable. Such a sense of irrational "otherness" is awesome and terrifying; often it is closely linked to the threat of death. Simultaneously, though, the religious symbol represents coherence, structure, and order in the world. It beckons with its assurance of all-embracing security. In this sense, it is related to the promise of continuing life. So religious symbols are paradoxical.... [T]o gain order and life we must accept, and perhaps experience intensely, disorder and death. The two are two sides of a single coin.[12]

Chernus claims that nuclear weapons represent the same two sides of this coin; chaos and order, death and life. Hence, the symbolic meanings of nuclear weapons (like the symbolic meanings of religion) are powerful and deeply embedded in a society's collective consciousness. This study, therefore, can illustrate the difficulties faced by those attempting to end society's dependence on these symbolically charged weapons (disarmament advocates), and can underscore the ultimate appeal of a technological solution that does not attempt to eliminate the *weapons*, but merely their destructive impact. SDI can be viewed as one example of such a technological solution.

In recent years, scholars have shown interest in the role of language in international relations and American foreign policy.[13] In the field of communication, studies in this area focus on two general questions: first, how does language shape foreign policy? Second, how does the rhetorical structure of American foreign policy stifle dissent and exclude opposing voices? This analysis of the rhetoric of SDI makes important contributions to present understanding in both of these areas. Also, it can provide important contributions to the current scholarship concerning SDI itself.

First, rhetorical studies concerned with exploring the relationship between language and foreign policy focus primarily on the examination of pro-war rhetoric as a genre of discourse. Robert L. Ivie analyzes American pro-war rhetoric and concludes that images of savagery are associated with the enemy in order to more easily assign guilt over the war to someone or some group other than the United States.[14] Others contribute to an understanding of such rhetorical structures by analyzing presidential justifications for involving the United States in various wars. Images of "aggression," "crisis," "force," and high moral purpose combine to create compelling rhetorical artifacts that persuade the American public to support war.[15]

All of these studies share an important assumption that is called into question when considered in light of SDI. These studies assume that the "enemy" in foreign policy rhetoric is clearly and concisely defined. Images of the "North Vietnamese," "the Chinese Communists," "the Soviet aggressors," "the savage Indian tribes," or any other enemy can be explained through these theoretical frameworks. But who (or what) is the enemy implied in pro-SDI rhetoric? The Soviet Union? The "Third World?" The nuclear bombs themselves? The scientists who created them? Ambiguity in pinpointing the enemy targeted by the Strategic Defense Initiative project seems to be strategically useful, in that the "true" objectives of the program are allowed to shift. For example, is SDI intended to be a complete population defense, protecting all American citizens from the evil enemy, the nuclear bomb itself? Or is SDI being developed in order to complicate any intended attack against United States' nuclear forces by the evil enemy, the Soviet Union? Or is SDI intended to allow the evil enemies, nuclear scientists, to atone for their sins of bringing atomic energy to the world? Each of these questions arises in an analysis of pro-SDI rhetoric. Exploring the concept of the enemy, and discussing the rhetorical and political implications of various constructions of the enemy adds to our understanding of foreign policy rhetoric.

In addition to analyzing images of the enemy in foreign policy discourse, scholars have attempted to explain the rhetorical elements of policy by studying various ways in which foreign policy events have been constructed symbolically in order to increase public support for government action. The Panama Canal Treaties, the "fall" of China, the rescue missions in Lebanon, the Dominican Republic and Grenada all have been the subject of rhetorical study.[16]

This study similarly attempts to place the rhetoric surrounding SDI into the context of pre-nuclear conceptions towards war and America's role in the global community. America's perceived mission to make the world safe for democracy, its quest to conquer new frontiers, and its "innocent" past all can be identified as underlying themes in pro-SDI rhetoric. In this sense, SDI, as a symbolic construction, hearkens back to America's past before the atomic bomb transformed consciousness. SDI attempts to bring America back to the past through the technology of the future.[17]

The second group of rhetorical studies of American foreign policy focuses on the way that foreign policy rhetoric entrenches the ideologies and power of elites and stifles dissenting voices. Philip Wander argues that symbolic constructions of America as a nation inherently stifle dissent over foreign policy.[18] The rhetoric of "prophetic dualism" (viewing enemies as the force of darkness and evil, and America as the force of light and goodness) stifles dissent, for who can argue against God and America's holy mission? Opponents of government policy in an age dominated by prophetic dualism are labeled heretics and traitors, thus rendered symbolically powerless. The rhetoric of "technocratic realism" (relying on America's technological base, sound management, and the advice of experts to guide foreign policy) stifles dissent, for who can argue with experts? In a world of experts, the opinions of the individual citizen about issues of grave national concern matter very little. From the perspective of technocratic realism, sound management, not public debate, is all that is needed for an effective foreign policy.

Other studies in this vein include G. Thomas Goodnight's lamentations over the separation of the personal, social, and technical spheres of argument, and his analysis of public discourse over the feasibility of civil defense.[19] In these studies, Goodnight argues that technical reasoning is essentially insulated from public moral argument. Given the logic of the scientific method, technical experts who participate in public policy decision making are not held strictly accountable for their policy proposals. T. K. Jones, for example, is able to argue for the feasibility of civil defense in the public policy arena based upon highly speculative technical reports. Even some of the most eloquent public policy arguers are not able to penetrate Jones' shield of technical reasoning. Goodnight argues that in this way, technical reasoning inhibits public debate on crucial national issues.

Walter R. Fisher's "narrative paradigm" represents an attempt to regain public accountability over technical reasoning and its products through a reconceptualization of all human communication as narration.[20] Fisher contends that the "rational world paradigm," which conceives of sound reasoning as rationalistic, clear-cut argumentative structures, more often than not excludes the average citizen from the realm of sound reasoning. Replacing the rational world paradigm with a new concept of reasoning, the narrative paradigm, brings the ordinary argumentation of the average citizen under the rubric of sound reasoning. Public moral argument, according to Fisher, is, therefore, every bit as "rational" as technical and scientific discourse. The insulation of technical reasoning from public accountability is especially relevant when examining nuclear rhetoric, given the highly technical nature of the weapons themselves and the aloof, esoteric nature of the language of strategic doctrine.

This study contributes to an understanding of these issues by examining a specific controversy that potentially further isolates the public from important foreign policy decisions. As a purely technological solution to the arms race, SDI seems to remove virtually *all* human intervention from this fundamentally moral and political problem. Deploying an antiballistic missile system in outer space removes the nuclear threat as far from human consciousness as is physically possible. As a result, does SDI cut off public debate over the morality of nuclear weapons? Is a technological solution to the arms race more appealing than a political or moral one? If so, why would Americans rather impose a questionable technological panacea than participate in a vigorous national debate over the wisdom and morality of the nuclear arms race? What role does public moral argument play in a technologically advanced society? I propose to provide some tentative answers to these questions.

Finally, I hope to further elaborate the symbolic understanding of SDI by building upon G. Thomas Goodnight's and Janice Hocker Rushing's analyses of Reagan's "Star Wars" address.[21] Goodnight examines Reagan's March 23, 1983 speech in the context of two previous addresses concerning national defense, the "Zero Option" speech and the "Evil Empire" speech. He concludes that SDI completes Reagan's attempt to create a rhetoric of war that predates Hiroshima, in that it offers an alternative to the arms race (which is immoral) and arms control (which is dangerous in an evil world). SDI is the only way out of the nuclear age, in this view, since the promise of arms control offered in the "Zero Option" speech cannot be kept, due to the existence of an "evil empire." Goodnight contends, however, that Reagan's vision fails, because he acknowledges in the "Star Wars" speech that coupling defensive systems with offensive weapons is highly destabilizing. Thus, Reagan's vision of the future is still fraught with the contradictions of the present.

Rushing presents an impressive analysis of the "Star Wars" speech. She argues that the address is an anomaly, in that it seemingly represents a victory of public discourse over the technical sphere. Reagan's non-technical view of SDI, she claims, defines the parameters for future technical debate in such a way that it constrains technical reasoning. Reagan is the author of the SDI drama, and the scientists merely actors, she claims. Scientists have but two choices: either accept Reagan's challenge to render nuclear weapons obsolete, and thereby give up the power to define their own purpose; or refuse the challenge, admit that science cannot solve this particular problem, and thereby undermine their own power.[22]

My approach builds upon these essays in several ways. First, by analyzing rhetorical artifacts since the March 23, 1983 speech, this study will examine the development of Reagan's and Bush's rhetorical stances towards SDI over time. As challenges and questions arose, both presidents were forced to modify their positions on SDI, and this study highlights those modifications. Second, this study not only analyzes presidential discourse, but also examines statements made by other administration officials. This important addition permits comparisons between technical and non-technical speakers within the Reagan and Bush Administrations, and provides insight into theoretical issues surrounding public and technical discourse. Third, exploring in more detail the contradiction pointed out by Goodnight in Reagan's original address, that defensive systems coupled with offensive systems are more destabilizing than offense alone, sheds light on the causes of this contradiction, as well as its implications for both advocates and opponents rhetorical stances. Fourth, this study challenges Rushing's claim that "Star Wars" represents the containment of technical reasoning by public discourse. I conclude that although Reagan may be the nominal author of this drama, his scientist-actors are modifying the script to fit it into their own language of technoscience. Their more limited version of SDI, as point defense, represents the way the program actually has been developed, not Reagan's vision of a complete population defense.

Method of Analysis

Although there are many useful ways for a critic of discourse to approach a set of texts, Kenneth Burke's dramatistic perspective on language informs my analysis. Since nuclear weapons and nuclear war are products of advanced technology and, therefore, symbol use, Burke's conception of symbols and their influence on human action is an appropriate perspective for a critic concerned with exploring these issues.[23] Burke's ontological assumptions, as revealed in his essay, *Definition of Man*, are grounded in symbol use. For Burke, the human being is:

> the symbol-using (symbol-making, symbol-misusing) animal
> inventor of the negative (or moralized by the negative)
> separated from his [sic] natural condition by instruments of his
>   [sic] own making
> goaded by the spirit of hierarchy (or moved by the sense of
>   order) and rotten with perfection.[24]

The use of language and the manipulation of symbols, Burke claims, separates human beings from other creatures. This ability allows humans to shape their environment and create reality through symbol use, and therefore, creatively respond to problematic situations as they arise. In an attempt to constantly improve the human condition and perfect the world, people use linguistic genius strategically to define situations in certain ways. Technology, Burke argues, is one manifestation of this "linguistic genius." Symbol use grants a degree of freedom to human beings, as they are able to manipulate their sense of reality to meet changing circumstances. But, paradoxically, the very freedom engendered by symbol use also creates constraints on human choice. Burke claims that symbolicity, responsible for conceptions of "the negative" and hierarchy, inevitably falls short of perfection, thus resulting in guilt. Therefore, although humans are free to shape reality through symbols, they must also suffer the consequences of symbol use: hierarchy, guilt, and alienation.

The use of language is action, according to Burke, since it is purposive and involves choice. It is purposive in that it serves to "form attitudes or to induce actions in other human agents."[25] The function of rhetoric for Burke, therefore, is "the use of language as a symbolic means of inducing cooperation in beings that by nature respond to symbols."[26] In order to explore more fully this function of rhetoric, Burke develops a philosophy of language called dramatism. If the essence of language use is action, as Burke maintains, then the most appropriate and complete metaphor to use to describe and evaluate language use is drama.[27]

A dramatistic perspective on the rhetoric of foreign policy is appropriate in that it focuses on the ritualistic and symbolic functions of language. In *Permanence and Change*, Burke argues that human beings, as social creatures, have a desire to order and interpret experiences to make sense of their world through symbolic identifications. The creation of a sense of order, or worldview, provides a degree of predictability in a changing and chaotic world.[28] As products of each individual's experiences and innermost thoughts, these worldviews are treated with great care and "piety" by the individuals who hold them.[29] When events threaten to shake the foundation of a worldview, humans react to re-create a sense of order. Burke argues:

> When a superstructure of certainties begins to topple, individual minds are correspondingly affected, since the mind is a social product, and our very concepts of character depend upon the verbalizations of our group.... At such a time, people naturally begin to look for some immovable `rock' upon which a new structure of certainties can be erected. The accepted terms of authority having fallen into disrepute, they seek in the cosmos or in the catacombs some undeniable body of criteria. They try to salvage whatever values, still intact, that may serve as the basis of new exhortations and judgments.[30]

Conceptions of the role of the United States in the global arena, as reflected in the nuclear arms race, represent such a structure of "certainties" having "fallen into disrepute," therefore, needing alteration or replacement by a new system of interpretation. The antinuclear movement, for example, challenged the authority of the status quo, naming it immoral and life-threatening. But, in SDI, Reagan proposed an alternative structure of "certainties," based on the appeal of American technological ingenuity, the historical experiences of the nation, and the hope of freeing Americans from the threat of nuclear peril.

Given a dramatistic perspective, any complete statement about discourse and its underlying motive will involve considerations of act, scene, agent, agency, and purpose, known collectively as the pentad. The "act" in discourse refers to any conscious or purposive action called for by the rhetor.[31] The "scene" is a term denoting location; the place, situation, or circumstance in which the act is grounded.[32] The "agent" is the person or group who is to carry out the act.[33] The "agency" is the tool or method to be used by the agent in carrying out the act, and the "purpose" is the explicit or implicit reason for performing the act.[34]

Burke explains that the pentad is analogous to one's hand. Each finger represents a separate element of the pentad, but they all come together in the palm of the hand.[35] The palm, therefore, represents the substance of the symbolic act, and each element of the pentad, if explored in depth, can lead the critic to the substance of the discourse.

When analyzing discourse from this point of view, the critic searches the text for accounts of these five dramatistic elements, and explores their interrelationships. This "grammar of motives" allows a critic to discover the strategic points where ambiguity arises in a text and, therefore, lends insight into the substance and motive underlying the discourse. By revealing and exploring how the rhetor dramatically shapes reality for him or herself, as well as for the audience, pentadic analysis provides an understanding necessary for critical statements about discourse. This approach will be explained further in chapter 4.

The texts I will analyze include public statements by Reagan, Bush, and officials in their administrations that attempt to explain and justify SDI. Primary sources for these texts include the *Weekly Compilation of Presidential Documents*, *The Department of State Bulletin*, the *U. S. Department of State Dispatch*, pamphlets and government documents written and released by the administration, testimony before congressional committees, and press releases and conferences. Since I am concerned with the Reagan and Bush Administrations' efforts to gain support for SDI, literature by non-administration sources concerning the potential applications of ballistic missile defense technologies will not be the primary focus of analysis.

The Historical and Rhetorical Context of SDI

Ever since the development of the atomic bomb, scientists, philosophers, policy makers, military strategists, and individual citizens have struggled to find a place for these weapons of mass destruction in America's foreign policy and sociocultural consciousness. The Truman administration, faced with this stunning new development that redefined American power in world affairs, "never worked out a clear strategy for deriving political benefits from its possession of nuclear weapons."[36] Once the Soviets acquired the bomb, the international situation became even more confusing and complex. Convinced of America's moral, spiritual, and political superiority, President Eisenhower developed a "New Look" of massive retaliation and brinksmanship, which contemplated the use of nuclear weapons in even small scale conflicts around the globe. As Eisenhower once said, the idea was "to blow the hell out of them in a hurry if they start anything."[37]

Apparently, this strategy was neither reassuring nor credible to the "new generation of Americans" who elected John F. Kennedy to the presidency. His strategy of "flexible response," financed through Keynesian economic policies, called for a military response at any and all levels of conflict, ranging from low-intensity conventional war to all-out nuclear war. Flexible response, as the jargon suggests, was intended to provide a policy maker with more choices "than humiliation or all-out nuclear war."[38] By late 1963, however, it became clear to administration officials that the doctrine's implied assumption of escalation control was implausible.[39] As a result, Robert McNamara's famous "MAD" doctrine—Mutual Assured Destruction—gradually became accepted as the official nuclear strategic policy of the United States.[40]

Since the mid-1960s, virtually all American presidents have relied upon the threat of retaliation as the foundation of their strategic nuclear policies.[41] The MAD doctrine, however, makes some crucial and increasingly challenged assumptions. First, it assumes that decision makers act "rationally" in times of both peace and crisis. No rational leader, according to the logic of MAD, would initiate a superpower confrontation knowing it would escalate to annihilation of both homelands. Second, MAD assumes that a situation of nuclear parity exists between the superpowers. If one state possesses significantly superior strategic forces, it might not be deterred from launching a preemptive nuclear strike in an attempt to destroy its opponent's retaliatory forces.

In 1981, Ronald Reagan took office convinced that nuclear parity no longer existed between the United States and the Soviet Union. While campaigning, he repeatedly emphasized the growing Soviet nuclear threat, arguing that a "window of vulnerability" undermined the stability of the strategic environment.[42] Between 1980 and 1985, Reagan embarked on the greatest peacetime military buildup in the history of the United States, increasing military expenditures by fifty-one percent after adjusting for inflation.[43] One-fourth of these expenditures were allocated for strategic modernization programs, focusing on the MX missile, the B-1 bomber, and the Trident submarine.[44]

This massive military buildup was accompanied by rhetoric that was increasingly belligerent and hostile toward the Soviet Union. This rejuvenation of the Cold War reached its zenith when Reagan, in a speech to Christian evangelicals in October, 1982, referred to the Soviet Union as an "evil empire" bent on world domination.[45] Although Reagan apparently was effective in persuading the public and Congress to modernize and upgrade nuclear forces, some observers argued that he was not quite as effective in discussing publicly issues of nuclear strategy, doctrine, and arms control. An excerpt from a Reagan news conference perhaps best illustrates this. When asked whether nuclear war could ever be kept limited, Reagan responded:

> Well, I would—if they realized that we—again if—if we led them back to that stalemate only because that our retaliatory power, our seconds, or strike at them after our first strike would be so destructive that they couldn't afford it, that would hold them off.[46]

It appears that Reagan was as confused as the average American citizen by the esoteric language, jargon, and logic embedded in the doctrine of mutual assured destruction. MAD depends upon paradoxes to fulfill its function of preventing nuclear war. For example, under MAD the United States and the Soviet Union must be willing to *use* nuclear weapons to guarantee that they are *never used*. States must *possess* nuclear weapons, and, in fact, continue to *build* them, in order to someday *eliminate* them. Citizens must put *faith* in the weapons that they *fear* so much. They must, as Chernus argues, worship the bomb because it will save them from the holocaust.[47] These paradoxical relationships arise out of humanity's attempts to make sense of a terrifying technological gadget that seems to transcend human abilities to comprehend its implications. Thus, the doctrine of deterrence, according to Jonathan Schell, is "the forbidding political and intellectual product of our attempt to live simultaneously in the two worlds—the nuclear, scientific world and the pre-nuclear military and political one."[48]

By 1980, the fatalism and frustration implicit in this situation erupted into a massive grassroots effort to redefine the role of nuclear weapons in America's defense posture: the nuclear weapons freeze campaign. A brief discussion of the rhetoric of nuclear freeze advocates is warranted to establish the symbolic context in which Reagan proposed SDI as an alternative vision of the future.

Various special interest groups in the United States have agitated for nuclear disarmament since the onset of the nuclear age. Groups such as the American Friends Service Committee (AFSC), the War Resisters League, the Women's International League for Peace and Freedom, and Clergy and Laity Concerned all have histories of protest against nuclear weapons. Paul Boyer argues that from 1963 to the 1970s, however, the voices of those opposed to the continued stockpiling of nuclear weapons were overwhelmed by several events. The Limited Test Ban Treaty of 1963 contributed to a perception of diminished risk; the immediacy of the nuclear threat abated as memories of Hiroshima and Nagasaki faded; the "peaceful" uses of atomic energy helped to neutralize the public's fears; and the complexity and reassurance of nuclear strategy created an apathetic public willing to cede control to experts.[49]

Such apathy held until 1980, when Randall Forsberg, founder of the Institute for Defense and Disarmament Studies and formerly of the Stockholm International Peace Research Institute, formulated a call for gradual disarmament that captured the attention of the entire nation. Her "Call to Halt the Nuclear Arms Race" was the first formal statement calling for a mutual freeze on the testing, production, and deployment of nuclear weapons by the United States and the Soviet Union.[50] This statement became the founding document of the nuclear freeze campaign, and set in motion a concerted grassroots effort to promote the freeze in municipalities in New England.

With the support of the AFSC, Quaker organizations and local activists, the word about the nuclear freeze proposal began to spread to the rest of the country. By the end of 1981, the freeze claimed 45,000 local organizers nationwide.[51] By March, 1982, over one million people in forty-three states were working to promote the freeze, and the resolution was on the ballot in five state referenda and innumerable local, city, and county elections.[52] A poll conducted by Yankelovich, Skelly, and White in March, 1982 found that seventy percent of those questioned favored a nuclear freeze.[53] It was clear that the freeze was a burgeoning grassroots campaign, beginning to influence state and local politics. Support for the resolution spread rapidly, and millions of citizens rallied around Forsberg's call to freeze the arms race.

Public concern permeated not only local government, but eventually reached the United States Congress. On March 16, 1982, Senators Edward Kennedy and Mark Hatfield introduced the nuclear freeze resolution into the Senate for consideration.[54] The same resolution was also introduced into the House of Representatives, and, as expected, created significant controversy. While the freeze resolution was being debated on Capitol Hill, public pressure mounted. On June 12, 1982, 750,000 Americans gathered in New York City to protest nuclear weapons, calling for a freeze and gradual disarmament. This was the largest political rally in the history of the United States, and it clearly illustrated the breadth of support for the freeze.[55]

The broad grassroots support for the freeze, however, did not translate officially into political success in Congress. In August, 1982, the House of Representatives narrowly defeated the nuclear freeze resolution by a vote of 204 to 202. Although the resolution failed, the narrow margin demonstrated to many freeze opponents the strength of this campaign, which they had earlier discounted. For example, the conservative *Arizona Republic* reported that "the slim two-vote margin...reveals just how sizeable the pro-freeze movement in the nation has suddenly become."[56] In addition, the narrow defeat served only to motivate supporters of the freeze to work even more diligently than before. Educational campaigns, local petition drives, and lobbying efforts were intensified, and a "scorecard" for rating House members support for the freeze and related issues was developed to aid sympathetic pro-freeze voters in their decisions.[57]

When a campaign such as the nuclear freeze begins to gather support and challenge the power and policies of the government, the prominent leaders of the establishment are forced to respond in some way to the challenge. Pressure continues to mount unless action is taken to respond to the agitators demands. The growing support for the nuclear freeze pressured the Reagan administration in this way. Those under attack, for example, were aware of the potential power of the antinuclear movement. George Yonas, chief scientist in charge of the Strategic Defense Initiative, stated:

> The opposition to MX and the freeze movement were very close to succeeding; the Catholic Bishops' pastoral letter...at one point said nuclear weapons were immoral. All of us working in the weapons game were aware of that whole business, including the anti-nuclear movement in Europe. There was a lot of frustration.[58]

Reagan's announcement of a national effort to research, develop, and eventually deploy a ballistic missile defense system can be viewed as a response to this frustration. It is important to consider SDI as an attempt both to respond to the growing pressure from the antinuclear movement and to symbolically create a sense of order in a MAD world. In his "Star Wars" address, for example, Reagan argued that MAD is "a sad commentary on the human spirit," and that America must "be capable of rising above dealing with other nations and human beings by threatening their existence."[59] Even if he did achieve verifiable arms control agreements, Reagan claimed, it would "still be necessary to rely on the specter of retaliation, on mutual threat" to maintain the peace.[60] But if the United States could use its technological ingenuity to develop a ballistic missile defense system that could destroy incoming missiles before they reached their targets, then it would render nuclear weapons "impotent and obsolete."[61] In this way, Reagan attempted to describe his SDI program as the most appealing solution to a public fearful and confused by the dangers of the arms race. SDI offered hope for eventually eliminating the nuclear threat, while a nuclear freeze would merely lock the superpowers into a stalemate.[62] Reagan's March 23, 1983 speech can be seen as a rhetorical response to a difficult political and symbolic situation. This speech set the stage for a substantial effort by the Administration to persuade Congress and the public to support the President's plan.

I contend that the Strategic Defense Initiative is rhetorically powerful for several reasons. First, Reagan effectively identified SDI with traditional American notions of destiny, mission, national innocence, and conquering new frontiers. By mustering these forces of patriotism and by identifying SDI with these deeply engrained American ideas, Reagan united his supporters with what he claimed were the greatest traditions in American history. Second, SDI effectively captured the symbolic appeal of the nuclear freeze proposal and nuclear disarmament. Touted as a way to make nuclear weapons impotent and obsolete, SDI seemed to offer a more complete solution to the nuclear dilemma than did proposals for gradual disarmament. Third, the Reagan Administration's SDI rhetoric, especially its claim that SDI was only a research project, created a symbolic niche for the program whereby it was insulated from strong criticism, and, simultaneously, was rhetorically self-perpetuating. Fourth, Bush's attempt to capitalize on the dramatic images of the Patriot anti-missile system during the Gulf War represented an appealing solution to the dangers inherent in the post-Cold War world: regional conflicts which threaten to escalate; the proliferation of weapons of mass destruction and ballistic missile systems; and accidental or terrorist launches of such weapons. Fifth, by offering a technological solution to these dangers, SDI removes human guilt and responsibility for the nuclear arms race, thus appearing to free humanity from the paradoxes associated with symbol use and its ultimate extension, technology itself. Such a technological solution, I argue, represents a surrender to what Burke calls the realm of motion, and is, therefore, an illusion of transcendence. These claims will be explored in the following chapters.

In chapter 2, the historical influences on pro-SDI rhetoric are revealed by exploring symbolic constructions of America's self-image as a morally superior nation, granted the divine destiny of creating peace and prosperity worldwide. This sense of destiny is evident in competing symbolic constructions of American history. I argue that these historical ideas influence SDI advocacy.

Chapter 3 traces the mounting public discontent in the United States in the 1980s over the nuclear arms race. I review the rhetorical strategies of advocates of the nuclear freeze proposal and the American religious community, in their attempts to challenge the Reagan nuclear arms buildup. I conclude that their collective rhetorical posture was vulnerable to a proposal like SDI.

Chapter 4 presents an analysis of the SDI rhetoric of the Reagan Administration. I argue that Reagan's SDI rhetoric tapped into the nation's historical sense of destiny, by proposing to conquer new frontiers with American technology and by providing a "non-aggressive" defensive solution to the arms race. In addition, SDI effectively captured the rhetorical appeal of the nuclear freeze proposal by promising to make nuclear weapons obsolete, without risking Soviet adventurism. Finally, I conclude that the Reagan Administration's SDI rhetoric effectively shielded the program from congressional scrutiny, while simultaneously providing it with momentum.

Chapter 5 is an analysis of the Bush Administration's attempts to justify SDI in an era of the collapse of the Cold War, increasing multipolarity in the international scene, the 1991 war in the Persian Gulf, and the rising concern with nuclear proliferation. I argue that the rhetorical structure of the Bush Administration's discourse is similar to Reagan's, in that the old "evil empire," the Soviet Union, has been replaced with new ones, personified by Saddam Hussein of Iraq. I conclude that the symbolic appeal of SDI is maintained, if not magnified, by this transference of the East-West rhetorical form to North-South issues.

Chapter 6 explores the pragmatic and theoretical implications of these symbolic readings of SDI. I argue that the SDI controversy illustrates the erosion of an ideal public sphere of discourse in two ways. First, SDI is a compelling example of presidential power manifested rhetorically, which serves to dominate public debate over foreign policy and quell dissent. Second, SDI represents a complete surrendering of the public sphere of discourse to technical rationality. Embracing technological solutions to the arms race removes the need for moral and political solutions, as well as the public debate required to formulate them.

2.
Innocence and Destiny in American Foreign Policy

IN A COMPLEX AND CHANGING WORLD, formulators and observers of American foreign policy interpret the problems facing the nation through the lens of past experience. Humans act in the present by calling upon knowledge that is shaped by the past; thus, the rhetorical meanings attributed to our national experiences throughout history can shed light on our present dilemmas, and our attempts to resolve them. One need only point to President George Bush's comparison of Saddam Hussein with Adolf Hitler, to understand the rhetorical force that conceptions of history can have in shaping symbolic constructions of policy. The history of U. S. foreign policy, viewed from a rhetorical perspective, consists of the viewpoints, accounts, explanations, and justifications that shape policy over time, that create a national identity, and that define America's role as a world actor.

In this chapter I argue that American policy makers have had a difficult time discarding the memories of the historical forces that have contributed to a "moralistic" view of American foreign policy. By this, I mean that a sense of moral superiority, shaped by heritage, and forged into a perception of a divine mission to free the world from evil and conflict, seems to dominate symbolic understandings of American foreign policy. This moralism is evident in various views of the proper role of the United States in world affairs, as they have recurred over the course of American history. This moral superiority pervades America's self-concept, I argue, and is part of its very identity as a nation.

To understand fully the rhetorical appeal of the Strategic Defense Initiative, it is necessary to survey some of these rhetorical constructions of the history of American foreign policy. Given my premise that the ability to make sense of present situations depends greatly upon a sense of the past, this historical survey can establish the rhetorical commonplaces that presently inform American perceptions of foreign policy. I do not pretend to construct a complete history of American foreign policy, nor do I pretend to have insight into a "true" interpretation of American history. All histories are in a sense revisionist, and this one is no exception.[1] My position is similar to Richard K. Ashley's, when he argued that history cannot be self-contained and attributed one fixed meaning. Rather, it is productive to view it "intertextually;" to consider various ways in which history is read, symbolically constructed, used to promote points of view, and to preserve various ideological and political interests.[2] My argument is that two of these "readings" have struggled for dominance in the public realm since the formation of the nation: isolationism and globalism. As symbolic, rhetorical constructions, isolationism and globalism serve as important interpretive frameworks for a discussion of the role of historical understanding in U. S. foreign policy.

The national experience of the United States, I will argue, seems to have contributed to a generalized self-image of innocence and moral superiority in a world dominated by conflict and rivalry. According to this view, America is destined to lead the world to a future of prosperity and peace. This moralistic perspective manifests itself in conceptions of both isolationism and globalism, which, I argue, share these notions of American moral superiority and national destiny, and which, in turn, shape contemporary interpretations of the Strategic Defense Initiative.

Early Conceptions of American Destiny

From the earliest moments of American history, a strong belief in "manifest destiny" is evident in the symbolic constructions of national character. Citizens of the New World conceived of themselves in a unique and even divine situation; they were chosen by God to create a society free from the conflict, struggle, and pain of the Old World. The Puritan pilgrims, fleeing religious intolerance in Great Britain, set out to create such a new society. As Hans Morgenthau pointed out:

the idea of America as the "chosen people" having a unique and divinely ordained mission to fulfill can of course be directly traced to Puritan England, to which an identical mission was attributed in identical terms. The Pilgrims brought that idea to America and used it unchanged in the American environment.³

John Winthrop, an early leader of the Massachussetts Bay Colony, called the settlement the "City upon a Hill," which was to become a theme echoed by generations of American leaders, from Thomas Jefferson to Ronald Reagan.⁴ To the Pilgrims, only divine Providence could have placed them in an environment of such plenty. Rich, fertile land and huge expanses of undeveloped terrain awaited them as they began their new lives. Although the winters were harsh and many died at first, the bountiful land soon bore fruit. In this new land there would be no need for conflict over resources, since there was plenty for all. The unpleasant aspects of life in Europe were left behind, and the settlers had a chance to forge a whole new beginning.⁵

The historical account of the "discovery" of America by Christopher Columbus, and the colonization of the area by the Pilgrims, served to obscure the fact that the "New World" was actually an old world for the indigenous native tribes inhabiting the land. Rendering the tribes symbolically nonexistent through a rhetoric of "discovery" paved the way for the conquest and slaughter that was to come later as the new nation expanded into the frontier.⁶ In any event, the Pilgrims sense of destiny enabled them to persist in difficult circumstances, notwithstanding the native inhabitants.

One should not underestimate the influence of religious dogma in contributing to this developing sense of destiny and mission among the new Americans. Reinhold Niebuhr argued that Calvinist theology influenced the Pilgrims belief that only people chosen by God could have been placed in a situation of such virtue and prosperity.⁷ From this belief it follows that if God created this land and these people, then it is the responsibility of these God-fearing people to help fulfill God's divine purpose: the creation of a society like no other. As Ralph Potter argued, "America was envisioned as the harbinger of the Kingdom of God on earth, a kingdom in which violence would not disrupt a new order built upon moral concord."⁸

It would be misleading to suggest that America is the only nation ever to conceive itself as engaged in a divinely inspired mission; in fact, most nations have done so at one point or another in their history.[9] Morgenthau claimed that the experience of the United States is unique, however, in that it is the only nation that established its purpose and mission *first*, before it had any national history which led to one.[10] In other words, both the Pilgrims and the founders of American independence had a purpose in mind when they set out to create a new society. Examining some of the beliefs of the "Founding Fathers" reveals the uniquely American characteristics of this sense of destiny. The political philosophies of Thomas Jefferson and Benjamin Franklin illustrate the secular and philosophical underpinnings of the belief in national destiny.

During the eighteenth century, Enlightenment philosophy spread throughout Europe. This "Age of Reason," particularly influential in France and England, saw human beings as essentially rational and good, capable of achieving perfection.[11] Philosophers from this school of thought believed, among other things, in natural law, a social contract, liberty, equality, progress, empiricism, and education.[12] They were intellectuals who were committed to improving the human condition through the application of reason to problems and by opposing tyrannical government.[13] Enlightenment philosophy exerted strong influence in the American colonies, in that it helped shape the political thinking of the more educated members of society, including Thomas Jefferson and Benjamin Franklin.

Jefferson's belief in natural law led to the optimistic assessment that humans are by nature good, moral, loving, and rational beings.[14] Jefferson, like his Pilgrim predecessors, concluded that "nature's god" must have had a special purpose in founding America: to make a new beginning in a corrupt and violent world.[15] As Lloyd Gardner, Walter LaFeber, and Thomas McCormick argued:

> [Jefferson] believed firmly that Americans were the new Chosen People, that they had been selected to found a more perfect nation that would be the political embodiment of John Winthrop's City Upon a Hill.[16]

Given the vast and potentially productive American frontier, Jefferson believed that the opportunity to create a community unscathed from the ravages of poverty, overpopulation, and want was at hand. In such a land of plenty, a community of virtue and prosperity consistent with the natural state of human beings was possible. Jefferson envisioned a decentralized, agrarian, democratic state as the most appropriate structure for this divine purpose. Only a state free from the corrupting influences of technology and specialization could preserve the destiny of the nation. In this society, disputes would be settled through moral persuasion, not force, and a natural state of peace and harmony would reign.[17]

Benjamin Franklin was not nearly as optimistic as Jefferson about the intrinsic goodness of human beings, but his commitment to the force of reason in human affairs resulted in similar conclusions about the destiny of the United States. Among eighteenth century philosophers, Franklin was considered to be the founder of American independence.[18] He believed that reason could temper human affairs, and that rational argument and scientific theories should govern social relationships. A democratic government, such as the newly created United States of America, called upon reason rather than coercion to guide the affairs of state. America, grounded as it was in reason, therefore, could hope somehow to banish coercion and strife from the world.[19] These notions formed the basis for Franklin's belief in America's "manifest destiny."[20]

Enlightenment philosophy, a European phenomenon, was adapted in these ways to fit conditions in America. As Henry Steele Commager put it, "the Old World imagined the Enlightenment and the New World realized it."[21] In the documents of the American Revolution, namely the Declaration of Independence and the United States Constitution, the ideals of the Age of Reason were enacted and institutionalized. The election of representatives to Congress, coupled with checks and balances, were to ensure that no one individual or branch of government could dominate policy making. Rather, reason, compromise, and spirited argument were assumed to result in decisions that were best for the new nation.

These notions of American destiny, grounded in religion and philosophy, combined to create a coherent body of "social knowledge" concerning America's role in the world.[22] Whether God, the great frontier, reason, or any combination of these was responsible for the nation's grand purpose, the sense of mission is evident in various conceptions of American foreign policy, ranging from the earliest moments in U. S. history to George Bush's call for a "new world order." Although Americans have disagreed about how this mission should be fulfilled, a sense of national superiority is one thread that can unify these competing interpretations of American history.

Moralism in American Foreign Policy

Early American foreign policy, if only due to geography, was grounded in neutrality and isolation from foreign conflicts. Given the expanse of the oceans and the western wilderness, the United States was fairly well-protected from the hostile influences of the great powers. Early American policy makers were concerned about preserving the political and military neutrality of the nation in order to supplement the natural protection provided by geography. In his "Farewell Address," President George Washington emphasized the importance of maintaining strict neutrality in political and military affairs when he stated:

> Why forego the advantages of so peculiar a situation? Why quit our own, to stand upon foreign ground? Why, by interweaving our destiny with that of any part of Europe, entangle our peace and prosperity in the toils of European ambition, rivalship, interest, humor, or caprice.... 'Tis our true policy to steer clear of permanent alliances with any portion of the foreign world.[23]

Washington hoped to persuade his immediate successors that active involvement in the affairs of the European states was unwise. The young nation needed to focus its attention inward, especially given its lack of effective seapower or military resources at the end of the Revolutionary War. The new national leadership hoped that the material wealth and abundance found in North America eventually would free the nation from the selfish motivations that commonly led to war in Europe. In a land of plenty, it seemed there would be no need for rivalry and conflict.

This land of plenty, of course, could produce great wealth and great quantities of mineral and agricultural products, which in turn could be sold to overseas markets. Early American revolutionaries, such as Thomas

Paine, in fact, saw the important economic benefits to be gained in overseas trade with the colonial powers.[24] Given the fear of political and military entanglements with Europe, however, the desire to increase economic ties was potentially problematic. How could the nation come to depend on international trade without its attendant political obligations? Early Presidents attempted explicitly to separate commercial concerns from political and military ones. Jefferson, for instance, claimed in 1801 that U.S. foreign policy could best be described as "peace, commerce, and honest friendship with all nations, entangling alliances with none."[25] This attempt to divorce questions of international trade from its political and military implications, however, was doomed to failure, as the expansion of the nation into the western frontiers would illustrate.

There were some powerful voices among early American leaders who claimed that expansion of the geographic boundaries of the nation was not only desirable, but necessary if the republic was to survive. James Madison argued in the Constitutional Convention that a democratic system of government required great expanses of land, in that diverse factions and interests, provided in part by geographic diversity, were needed to balance and counterbalance one another.[26] Jefferson agreed, in that a primarily agrarian society needed large expanses of land to support the export of products overseas.[27] Franklin argued in his so-called "population theory" that the key to success as an independent nation was to increase the birth rate. As more Americans were born, national affluence would grow and with it an ability to challenge the colonial power of Great Britain.[28] Franklin's theory proved to be accurate, as increasingly more American settlers began to migrate west in the early 1800s. The expansion of the nation to the Mississippi River and beyond, culminating in the Louisiana Purchase, set the stage for this mass migration into the frontier. As the U. S. expanded its boundaries, however, it inevitably encountered opposition from the dominant colonial powers of the time; France, Spain, and Great Britain.

The Monroe Doctrine of 1823 directly challenged these European powers in the western hemisphere by claiming, "The American Continents...are henceforth not to be considered as subjects for future colonization by any European powers."[29] Implicitly, of course, this statement encouraged *American* expansion into the frontier, and the acquisition of Texas, California, and the Oregon territories by the United States was soon to follow.[30]

This westward migration was caused by many factors, including population pressures, the desire to expand overseas markets (including Asian ones, thus, the need for strong port cities in Oregon and California), and increasing industrialization in northern cities.[31] But, the ideological affiliations of a peculiarly American sense of mission became attached to this migration as more and more commentators noted the confluence of geographic expansion with American ideas and values. As Frederick Jackson Turner wrote:

> This perennial rebirth, this fluidity of American life, this westward expansion with its new opportunities, its continuous touch with the simplicity of primitive society, furnishes the forces dominating American character...[32]

These "forces dominating American character" included for Turner, values such as democracy, individualism, and nationalism, while others included social Darwinist ideas of the survival of the fittest, Anglo-Saxon racism, and Christian doctrine to explain and justify this building of an empire.[33] In any case, it became clear that the United States would not be aloof from political and military entanglements with Europe, as it became a global power both in terms of geographic size and economic clout.

During the last third of the nineteenth century, the United States seemed to be fulfilling its material destiny, as commerce and prosperity flourished. From 1861 to 1901, notwithstanding the depression of 1890, the United States became the leading industrial and agricultural producer in the world.[34] By conquering the western frontier, the prosperity promised by the Pilgrims and Jefferson became a reality for more and more Americans. By the turn of the century, the United States was emerging as a global economic power, and the expansion of foreign trade eventually began to influence the rhetorical battle over the proper role of the nation in the world.

As economic growth continued, the United States gradually became inextricably tied to the affairs of other nations. As American corporations expanded, so did trade with European powers and their colonies. But American economic expansion did more than simply create commercial ties with other nations; it also contributed to a gradual redefinition of America's destiny in the world. No longer perceiving themselves as merely citizens of an aloof, independent, shining example of democracy, more and more Americans were attracted to a rhetoric of crusading American imperialism.

Perhaps the most vivid example of this new American myth of destiny in action was the Spanish-American War of 1898. Conscious of the presence of the Spanish empire in the Caribbean and the Pacific, the United States set out to "liberate" Cuba, Puerto Rico, and the Philippines from Spanish hegemony. The Old Empire, motivated by greed and imperialism, was to be replaced by the New Empire, motivated by righteousness, freedom, and progress.[35] Some advocates of this new global imperialism perceived the motives for American expansion as noble and righteous, in contrast to the ignoble motives of the fading, corrupt empires of Britain and Spain. Others argued that increased U. S. presence in the Caribbean and the Pacific was necessary to ensure both military security and economic expansion into Asian markets.[36]

As economic prosperity continued during the early days of the twentieth century, so did the rhetoric of American imperialism. The dominant voice of United States imperialism, beginning with the Spanish-American War, was Senator Albert J. Beveridge.[37] His crusading rhetoric called for the nation to continue to expand beyond its borders, carrying the American flag and the torch of democracy with it.[38] At least in the Western Hemisphere, this rhetoric of imperialism took shape in Theodore Roosevelt's Big Stick diplomacy. His dealings with the nation of Panama, which eventually separated from Colombia in order to facilitate construction of the canal, represented a merger of the rhetoric of crusading imperialism and the power of American economic interests. By the turn of the century, the United States had become a great world power, in word and in deed.

Although a long period of relative isolation had come to an end, the vast majority of Americans still clung, ironically, to a sense of neutrality, at least toward the nations of Europe.[39] Apparently economic involvement, such as Taft's "Dollar Diplomacy" and even wholesale diplomatic and military interference in Nicaragua and Mexico by Taft and Wilson, could not shake the prevailing public understanding of America's neutrality.[40] It was at this moment in American history that the rhetorical struggle over the role of the United States in world affairs became most evident. Americans clung to the inherited symbolic appeal of isolation and neutrality, even though other symbolic constructions of the economic, political, and even military conditions of the time were not consistent with the isolationist view.

This struggle to maintain a rhetoric of neutrality became more and more difficult as war broke out in Europe. Examining the responses by American policy makers to the beginning of World War I reveals how deeply embedded isolationism was in the American consciousness. Wilson was reluctant to get involved in the war, claiming it was merely another example of selfish power rivalries erupting into war in the Old World. Even though he earlier ordered U. S. troops into Mexico to overthrow Victoriano Huerta and bolster the stability of U. S. investments there, he believed that somehow European colonialism was more troublesome than American. Our nation was above the petty power rivalries of Europe, claimed Wilson, as he urged Congress to maintain neutrality in August, 1914:

> this great country of ours, which is, of course, the first in our thoughts and in our hearts, should show herself in this time of peculiar trial a Nation fit beyond others to exhibit the fine poise of undisturbed judgment, the dignity of self control, the efficiency of dispassionate action; a Nation that neither sits in judgment upon others nor is disturbed in her own counsels and which keeps herself fit and free to do what is honest and disinterested and truly serviceable for the peace of the world.[41]

Norman Graebner revealed Wilson's belief in the historical destiny of the nation, when he claimed that Wilson "conceived of the United States as a nation uniquely endowed to lead the world out of the jungle of war into a new era of peace in which law and reason would govern the behavior of nations..." Wilson argued that the world would turn to the U. S. for moral leadership, because "her flag is the flag not only of America, but of humanity."[42]

Once again, the language of mission and neutrality appeared in statements of American foreign policy. As Ronald Steel pointed out, some citizens were convinced of America's aloofness from the power rivalries of the European continent, while others were immigrants of German and Irish descent, who opposed involvement on the side of the Allies. By 1916, "Isolationist sentiment was still too powerful and public suspicion of Allied imperialism too great. A British Empire that kept India in bondage and had brutally repressed the Easter uprising in Ireland did not seem, to many Americans, worth preserving."[43]

But public sentiment for neutrality did not translate into a neutralist policy. Although the United States remained officially neutral, its trading policies greatly favored the Allies. From 1914 to 1916, the United States traded food, raw materials, and munitions to the Allied powers.[44] J. P. Morgan arranged loans for Britain through American banks, which enabled an economically drained alliance to continue the war effort. Whether these economic policies were the result of concerted efforts by "merchants of death" (Wall Street financiers and munitions plant owners) to get the nation involved in the war, as some argued, or the result of America's dependence on British sea power for its commerce, they eventually led to active United States involvement.[45]

The presidential campaign of 1916 pointed to the complexities involved in the continuing rhetorical battle between advocates of internationalism and advocates of isolationism. The Republican party was faced with internal dissent, as Theodore Roosevelt's Bull Moose faction actively promoted United States involvement in international affairs.[46] The party's presidential nominee, Charles Evans Hughes, aware of strong public sentiment on the side of continued neutrality, attempted to moderate the Republican position. Hughes himself advocated "true" neutrality, calling for the elimination of favorable treatment of the Allies.[47] This position won him favor with German- and Irish-American voters, who construed Wilson's neutrality as blatantly pro-British.

Given Roosevelt's public endorsement of Hughes, however, Wilson was able to effectively identify Hughes with the pro-war internationalist faction of the Republican party. Claiming that a vote for Hughes was a vote for war, Wilson seized the opportunity to establish himself as the candidate of peace.[48] Arthur Link argued that anti-war sentiment, which was running high in the midwest and west and was not decidedly partisan in nature, allowed Wilson to be reelected primarily on the basis of his peace platform.[49]

All this is not to say, however, that Wilson's anti-war position was equivalent to the earlier rhetorical appeal for isolation from foreign entanglements. On the contrary, Wilson was calling publicly for a new internationalism, an internationalism based upon a world organization joined together to preserve the peace. During the 1916 campaign he called for the establishment of a postwar league of nations, arguing that in the modern world neutrality was difficult to maintain.[50] Although Wilson wished to maintain American neutrality in World War I for as long as possible, he envisioned a future American globalism which would ensure the peaceful settlement of all disputes. Hence, Wilson's rhetoric of peace was not merely a rhetoric of isolationism, but rather a vision of neutrality for the short term, with active international involvement in the immediate postwar period. Wilson's position was appealing to many anti-war voters, for it promised peace in the present as well as long into the future. Or, as Graebner argued, Wilson's perspective on world stability was appealing because it promised preservation of the status quo without the risks of involvement in power politics all around the globe.[51]

Given the long-standing appeal of the rhetoric of neutrality, some equally appealing justification for active American involvement in the war was necessary, once this involvement became unavoidable. German attacks on merchant ships and civilian liners on the high seas provided it. The sinking of the British liner *Lusitania* on May 7, 1915 and the subsequent drowning of 128 American citizens, produced moral outrage in the United States.[52] Several American merchant vessels were attacked as well, culminating in the destruction of three American ships in March, 1917.[53] It became increasingly clear that Wilson could no longer uphold neutrality. War with Germany seemed inevitable as members of the public demanded vindication of American rights to travel in international waters.[54] Although the nation was bitterly divided over the question of whether the United States should declare war against Germany, the pro-war voices were growing louder and stronger as attacks on neutral ships continued. Eventually Wilson was forced to abandon neutrality and call for a declaration of war.

Proclaiming the noble purpose of defending the freedom of the seas, Wilson addressed the Congress on April 2, 1917. He echoed the outrage felt by Americans when he argued:

> There is one choice we cannot make, we are incapable of making: we will not choose the path of submission and suffer the most sacred rights of our nation and our people to be ignored or violated. The wrongs against which we now array ourselves are no common wrongs; they cut to the very roots of human life.[55]

Ironically, the nation which pledged in 1914 to exercise sound judgment and vigilant self-control was, in 1917, embroiled in a moral crusade to restore the rights of all humankind. The moralistic rhetoric of isolation and neutrality was translated into the moralism of a war to make the world safe for democracy. Wilson attempted to maintain the pure and virtuous moral purpose of the United States, however, when he asserted, "We have no selfish ends to serve. We desire no conquest, no dominion.... We are but one of the champions of the rights of mankind."[56] Barbara Tuchman and others contended that Wilson was personally committed to exerting moral leadership in a world at war. He wanted to serve humanity through what he believed to be the moral force of the United States.[57]

By entering World War I, the United States therefore officially broadened its mission. No longer isolated from the rivalries, arms races, and wars of the European continent, America was to fight a war to free the world from those very evils. A rhetorical construction of moral isolationism rather quickly became translated into one of moral globalism.[58] Realizing that isolationism was merely a nostalgic and naive posture in a world at war, the United States committed itself to the use of force to fulfill its divine destiny of creating a world of self-determination and one free from war and strife.

As World War I drew to a close, the brutality of modern warfare became all too evident. Wilson's League of Nations was an attempt to transfer into the diplomatic and legal arenas the moral zeal with which America fought the war. In other words, the League of Nations was conceived as a means for outlawing war altogether, thus, creating the peaceful and prosperous utopia promised by America's destiny. But once integrated into the Treaty of Versailles, the League of Nations was doomed to failure. The Senate's rejection of the treaty can be explained in several ways. Ralph Stone argued that elements of the treaty providing for war reparations and territorial divisions offended liberal supporters of the League to such an extent that they voted against the entire treaty, including the League of Nations.[59] W. Stull Holt claimed that party politics killed the treaty; the Republicans, led by Henry Cabot Lodge, attached so many reservations that the treaty was essentially gutted.[60] Whatever the causes, however, rejection of the League of Nations effectively ended Wilson's hopes for a permanent postwar peace.

In the period between the World Wars, the United States attempted to revert back to isolationism. Graebner argued that this was evident in lingering Wilsonian desires for moral and legal alternatives to war and in Congressional actions designed explicitly to maintain U. S. neutrality in the mid-1930s.[61] Even though World War I was an unmistakable sign that the nation could no longer be free from conflicts in Europe, the language and attitude of isolationism was a familiar and reassuring theme for many Americans. Some citizens undoubtedly embraced isolationism out of a sense of nostalgia for the "good old days," when the United States was free from concern about the affairs of other nations. Given the horrific nature of World War I, such a longing for the innocence of the past is understandable.[62] Perhaps others returned to isolationism as a way of preserving American prosperity. Internationalism in the postwar period meant sharing America's good fortune with others, an idea that did not appeal to some Americans.[63]

In any event, the onset of the Great Depression effectively forced the attention of the nation inward, as Franklin Delano Roosevelt struggled to rebuild the American economy in the 1930s. The national mythology of prosperity for all and progress forever was shattered as millions became unemployed. As the efforts of the nation were focused inward, tensions rose, and conflict once again broke out on the European continent. When World War II broke out in Europe, the nation once again officially attempted to maintain neutrality for as long as possible. Signs of impending U. S. involvement were evident as early as 1937 when Roosevelt argued in his "Quarantine Speech" that there would be "no escape through mere isolation and neutrality."[64] But, direct U. S. participation in the war was not to come until four years later. In fact, James McCormick claims that there was virtually no major United States involvement in the war until the attack on Pearl Harbor on December 7, 1941, proclaimed by Roosevelt as "a day that will live in infamy."[65]

As in the First World War, once involved, the United States pursued its objectives with missionary zeal. Hitler's march through Europe "rekindled the spirit of America's sense of mission, which sought to serve the interests of all humanity" by crushing tyranny and establishing freedom.[66] Moral combat against the forces of evil once again defined the execution of the war effort. In contrast to World War I, however, the officially stated and desired outcome of World War II, from the American perspective, was unconditional surrender, total war, and annihilation of the enemy.[67] Roosevelt was determined to avoid what he considered to be the main mistake of World War I; allowing for a negotiated peace. Roosevelt was convinced that the military and economic might of Germany and Japan had to be crushed to prevent them from rising again and starting World War III.[68] While the United States entered World War I without the intention of conquest or dominion, it did so for the ultimate moral purpose of restoring human rights to all nations. This logic merely was carried one step further in America's effort during the Second World War. Not only were the purposes ultimate (stopping the evil of facism), but so were the means necessary for the achievement of those purposes (annihilation).

Thus, the supreme irony of America's destiny emerged: the moralistic rhetoric that precluded involvement in the affairs of other nations was transformed into a rhetoric that justified a complete lack of restraint once war was unavoidable. Once the "ethic of the saint"—innocent and aloof—became transmuted into the "ethic of the holy crusader"—involved and committed—emergency measures, such as the bombings of Dresden, Tokyo, Hiroshima, and Nagasaki, were rhetorically justified.[69] When the nation fought to defend ultimate values, ultimate measures were appropriate. As James Hikins has argued, the crusading rhetoric of unconditional surrender ultimately constrained policy choices and contributed to the use of atomic weapons twice against Japan.[70]

The United States emerged from World War II undoubtedly the strongest nation on earth and inevitably an active player in international politics. Possessing a monopoly on the atomic bomb, and faced with a mortal threat from a hostile ideology, the nation could no longer afford to return to the security and safety of its isolationist past. The United States was forced to either carve out a new symbolic conception of its role in the world or creatively forge a view that was consistent with its historical mission and destiny. Some of the scientists involved in the Manhattan Project attempted to create an alternative view of America's role: one as founder of a world government that would maintain centralized control over atomic energy.[71] But, as the Soviet Union acquired atomic weapons, and Stalin's "Iron Curtain" descended around Eastern Europe, this vision of international cooperation faded.

On February 22, 1946, George Kennan's "long telegram" was dispatched from Moscow. In this document, Kennan argued that the Stalin regime and indeed the whole Soviet system depended upon suspicion and hostility towards the West, in order to sustain itself. As a result, Kennan argued, friendly relations with the U. S. S. R. would not be possible. The entire foundation of American diplomacy regarding the Soviet Union would have to be changed. Isolationism was no longer an option for the United States; the policy dispute in the post-1945 period centered instead on how best to implement Kennan's call for "containment" of Soviet expansionism. Originally conceived as predominantly a diplomatic and economic strategy, containment soon became part of a more compelling rhetorical stance, one fed by fear, mistrust, and secrecy: the Cold War.[72]

The crusading rhetoric of the Cold War, with its emphasis on the inevitable confrontation between the forces of light and the forces of darkness, merged nicely into the historical rhetoric of destiny in American history.[73] America's mission of creating a world of prosperity and virtue could only be achieved in a world free from the communist menace. Democratic nations, not totalitarian dictatorships, represented the ideal future of humankind; therefore, the United States was forced to act to contain Soviet expansionism. Rather than isolate itself from the dirty work of international politics, passively waiting for the rest of the world to crumble at its feet, the United States had to take an active part in guaranteeing the survival of democracy in a hostile world. Its sense of destiny preserved by the rhetoric of the Cold War, the nation set out to do battle with communist insurgencies around the globe, ultimately leading to wars in Korea and Vietnam.

The globalization of U. S. security interests had its roots in the Truman Doctrine of March, 1947, in which the commitment to intervene anywhere in the world to prevent the spread of communism was codified. Dean Acheson claimed in 1950 that:

> The interests of the United States are global in character.... A threat to the peace of the world anywhere is a threat to our security."[74]

In June of that year, this thinking contributed to the deployment of U. S. troops to the Korean Peninsula. Similarly, in a 1954 press statement, Eisenhower spoke of the communist threat posed by Ho Chi Minh in Vietnam, arguing that the United States must stand firm, for if one more nation in Southeast Asia fell, all the others would follow, like a row of dominoes.[75]

But neither the Korean nor the Vietnam War lived up to the glorious expectations created by the crusading rhetoric of anticommunism. American efforts in Korea, fueled by expectations of total victory, were frustrated by limited objectives and the continual threat of escalation to nuclear war.[76] Vietnam was anything but an archtypal heroic crusade against Soviet expansionism; combatants and noncombatants were indistinguishable in a civil war that turned into a quagmire.

The failure of the war effort in Vietnam stunned the nation, and at least temporarily shattered its commitment to moral globalism.[77] Nixon's and Kissinger's embrace of realism and power politics can be viewed as a reaction against undue moralism in American foreign policy. In fact, some have called Nixon's foreign policy "fundamentally amoral."[78] But the nation's flirtation with realism was not to last; Jimmy Carter was elected to the presidency on a platform calling for the restoration of morality in foreign affairs.[79] When Ronald Reagan occupied the White House, he returned to the moralistic rhetoric of the Cold War.[80] And George Bush proclaimed the dawning of "a new world order...in which the nations of the world, East and West, North and South, can prosper and live in harmony."[81]

In the period since the end of World War II, the United States has struggled to make sense out of its new role of global responsibility in a world of rivalry, conflict, and power politics. As Neibuhr puts it: "Our dreams of a pure virtue are dissolved in a situation in which it is possible to exercise the virtue of responsibility toward a community of nations only by courting the prospective guilt of the atomic bomb."[82] In a Burkean sense, symbol use, culminating in the development of tools and technology, has led America to a situation in which order is preserved only by threatening the obliteration of order and symbol use itself, that is, nuclear annihilation. America's dreams of innocence and virtue, grounded in historical experience, are clouded by the guilt inherent in symbol use and its ultimate manifestation, nuclear weapons.

It is clear that various interpretations of American history, with their corresponding beliefs in national destiny, will always be present. America cannot free itself from the legacy of the past. Only through the creative use of symbols can the nation attempt to integrate the events of the past into the demands of the present and the hopes for the future. This is no easy task, given the complexities of international security in the nuclear age. As Morgenthau wrote:

> Yet by weighing the inescapable risks of the atomic age against a riskless past and futilely trying to restore it, America has posed itself midway between the past and the future. With its mind's eye, it beholds the needs of the future; yet it wishes for the return of a past that is forever lost. Thus, its purpose to provide for its survival in a surviving world is blurred, and its designs, bold and forward-looking in themselves, are in execution chained to a past that is dead.[83]

The United States is caught between its mythology of national innocence and virtue and its possession and use of the ultimate destructive weapon. Can the use of language function to relieve this national guilt? Given that language use engenders hierarchy, guilt, and eventually disorder, how can humanity escape from the implications of its symbol-laden condition? Can the United States regain lost innocence by somehow returning to a pre-nuclear and pre-symbolic state? Given a democratic system of government, which is based inevitably on the rhetorical precept that moral persuasion is preferable to brute force, is it possible, or even desirable, to face these dilemmas through public moral argument? Or does the promise of technology and science—the second American frontier—offer a more plausible and sure solution to the nuclear arms race? In the next three chapters, I examine the rhetorical interaction between the anti-nuclear movement and the campaign for ballistic missile defense systems, and the Persian Gulf War, to suggest tentative answers to these questions.

3.
Rhetorical Challenges
to the Arms Race

RONALD REAGAN'S ELECTION to the presidency in 1980 represented to many proof of a public desire to reassert American military power in the world. The "malaise" of the Carter years, the Iran hostage crisis, the Soviet invasion of Afghanistan, and the fading memories of the Vietnam War all contributed to a feeling that the United States was no longer the world's strongest superpower. Reagan campaigned on a platform that called for massive increases in military spending, and, once elected, he proceeded to follow through on his promise to rebuild America's defenses.

Support for Reagan's defense buildup, however, was by no means universal. Almost simultaneously with Reagan's election, public activism against the nuclear arms race grew. In the early 1980s, many American citizens worked actively to educate themselves and their neighbors about the dangers of the nuclear arms race. The nuclear weapons freeze campaign, which reached its pinnacle in 1982, was described as the most powerful social movement in the United States since the Vietnam War era, and was the twentieth-century counterpart to Abolition.[1]

Antinuclear weapons activism in the early years of the Reagan Administration challenged the nuclear buildup that Jimmy Carter began and Reagan vigorously pursued. As the strength of the freeze campaign grew, so did the rhetorical challenges faced by the administration. George Yonas, formerly the chief scientist in charge of the Strategic Defense Initiative, expressed the concern felt by the Reagan Administration:

> The opposition to MX and the freeze movement were very close
> to succeeding; the Catholic Bishops' pastoral letter [on war and

peace]...at one point said nuclear weapons were immoral. All of us working in the weapons game were aware of that whole business, including the antinuclear movement in Europe. There was a lot of frustration.[2]

The administration, leading a nation with a historical self-image of high moral purpose, therefore, faced a difficult rhetorical situation that demanded a strong response.

This chapter traces the development of various rhetorical challenges to the nuclear arms race in the early 1980s. I begin with a brief discussion of the history of antinuclear weapons protest in the United States. Then, I trace the development of the nuclear weapons freeze campaign, and argue that five main themes were present in the discourse of freeze supporters: faith in common sense; fear of nuclear war; concern about nuclear overkill; a sense of urgency; and impatience with traditional arms control. Finally, I conclude with a critical analysis of pro-freeze discourse, and contend that it was rhetorically vulnerable to a proposal like Reagan's Strategic Defense Initiative.

Early Reactions to Atomic Weapons

To appreciate fully the strength of the nuclear freeze campaign's challenge to the Reagan buildup, it is helpful to explore public reactions to nuclear weapons prior to 1980. At the end of World War II, after the United States used nuclear weapons twice against Japan, Americans attempted to make sense of these weapons and somehow explain the impact they would have on future generations. These early responses to atomic weapons, I argue, set the foundation for later interpretations which are still evident today.

The most dominant public response to the beginning of the nuclear age was relief that these new and terribly destructive weapons had brought World War II to an end. One popular account justifying U. S. actions at Hiroshima and Nagasaki, the one advocated by President Truman, held that the United States had to use the atomic bomb to bring a quick end to the war and to save American lives. A Gallup poll taken in August, 1945 revealed that eighty-five percent of those surveyed approved of the use of atomic weapons against Japan, and a Roper poll a few months later revealed that seventy-six percent either approved of the decision or believed that the United States should have used more bombs before Japan had a chance to surrender.[3]

Truman, defending his decision to use the bomb against Hiroshima, argued that his administration deliberately chose this city because it was primarily a military, not civilian, target.[4] The intent of the attack, therefore, was to deal a final and decisive blow to Japan's ability to continue waging war against the Allies. The dominant public justification for the use of the bomb, of course, was that many more lives, Japanese and American, would have been lost if the Allies attempted an invasion of Japan. This explanation seemed quite compelling to a nation weary of war, and as Paul Boyer argued, it fundamentally shaped American public opinion toward the bombings of Hiroshima and Nagasaki.[5]

A second interpretation of the meaning of the atomic age began to take shape as early as 1946, when more detailed news of the awful destruction in Japan reached the United States. Claiming that the bomb was a blessing in disguise, some argued that all of its terrible implications somehow would force humankind to renounce war as an instrument of politics. This precursor to the doctrine of Mutual Assured Destruction (MAD) was exemplified by Louis Ridenour's claim that the atomic bomb "holds some promise of being, at last, the instrument which will cause nations to renounce war as a means of adjusting differences."[6] Some commentators, like Nathaniel Peffer, went even further, claiming that citizens should embrace the onset of the nuclear age:

> Indeed, it is not just Swiftian satire to say that if there must be war again it had better be fought with atomic bombs. The end will be quicker and more merciful. The need to prevent war and the question whether it can be prevented have taken on a new urgency.[7]

The acceptance of nuclear weapons precisely because of their destructive potential set the foundation for some contemporary views of nuclear deterrence. According to one school of thought, if sufficient retaliatory forces could survive a surprise attack, the hypothetical adversary would be deterred from initiating the attack in the first place. Given such assumptions, it would seem that no action was required to end the production of nuclear weapons. In a way, the problem would take care of itself; the existence, and even the continued production, of the weapons guaranteed that they would never be used. If these assumptions were granted, public apathy concerning the risks involved in the arms race would be a likely response. Boyer observed, in fact, that such a sense of public helplessness began to appear as early as 1946. He argued that genuine support for the nuclear buildup as a way to promote peace, combined with apathy about the risks involved in such a buildup, discouraged public activism against nuclear weapons.[8]

A third public response to the beginning of the nuclear age emerged through voices of protest against the use of atomic weapons in Japan. Expressing this viewpoint, the editorial board of the *New York Herald Tribune* wrote that Hiroshima and Nagasaki represented "the greatest simultaneous slaughter in the whole history of mankind," and compared American actions to those of Nazi Germany.[9] Some religious leaders echoed this condemnation of the atomic bombings. Harry Emerson Fosdick of New York City's Riverside Church contended:

> When our self-justifications are all in, every one of us is nonetheless horrified at the implications of what we did. Saying that Japan was guilty and deserved it, gets us nowhere. The mothers and babies of Hiroshima and Nagasaki did not deserve it.[10]

The Federal Council of Churches of Christ formed the Calhoun Commission in March, 1946, to formulate the first official church statement regarding the morality of nuclear weapons. Although the Commission concluded that the attacks against Hiroshima and Nagasaki were immoral and unjustified, it remained divided over whether all potential future uses of nuclear weapons also would be immoral.[11] Neither Catholic, Protestant nor Jewish officials categorically condemned the future use of atomic weapons in the early stages of the nuclear age, thereby failing "to render a clear and unequivocal no to these new instruments of mass destruction."[12]

Some, however, did attempt to say no to nuclear weapons. Ironically, one vocal group consisted of those who helped bring atomic weapons into the world. What came to be known as "the scientists' movement," which included many members of the Manhattan Project, worked to block attempts at placing all atomic research under military control, and lobbied for the establishment of an international agency to control atomic energy research and development.[13] After several years of lobbying and educational campaigns, however, the scientists failed to bring a halt to the burgeoning nuclear arms race.

In the early 1950s, with the entrenchment of the Cold War and the Soviets' acquisition of nuclear weapons and satellite technology, public activism against the arms race diminished. Boyer contended that vocal protest against above-ground testing of nuclear weapons (which emerged in 1962 in response to the detection of strontium 90 in milk), and a flurry of activism in the late 1960s concerning antiballistic missile proposals, are the only exceptions to a long period of public acquiescence to nuclear weapons policies.[14] It was not until the early 1980s that strong, grassroots protests reemerged to challenge the authority of the government to continue to escalate the arms race.

The Nuclear Weapons Freeze Campaign

After thirty-five years of nuclear weapons production and deployment, very little sustained public opposition to the arms race was evident. In 1980, however, public interest and involvement concerning the issue grew steadily, culminating in a national campaign to freeze the arms race. Undoubtedly, many factors contributed to the strength of this campaign, among them the Reagan Administration's push to build accurate new weapons systems like the MX missile, the B-1 bomber, and the Trident II submarine, the decision to deploy cruise missiles in the European theater, and growing antinuclear activism in Europe. Although the advent of new military hardware was undoubtedly influential in providing an impetus for antinuclear weapons protest, I argue that the rhetorical posture of the administration was an important factor that motivated people into action. Three examples illustrate this: the administration's attempts to explain publicly its interpretations of nuclear strategy; its calls for civil defense relocation plans at the local level; and its increasingly belligerent tone toward the Soviet Union.

Charles-Philippe David argued that the evolution of the United States nuclear strategy can be viewed as a struggle between two alternative perspectives.[15] One view holds that since nuclear weapons are fundamentally different than conventional arms, developing detailed war plans for their use is naive and even risky. This interpretation assumes that the mere threat of retaliation guarantees peace through deterrence. Attempts to make nuclear weapons seem usable, according to this view, are inherently destabilizing since they would make nuclear war "thinkable" and, therefore, more likely. The other view holds that prudent planners should carefully work out ways to use nuclear weapons in a controlled fashion, should deterrence fail. Since the threat of retaliation must be credible, and since U. S. planners need an ability to act at various levels of the "escalation ladder," this view attempts to place nuclear weapons squarely within viable operational and tactical practices. Some analysts claim that since 1974, when the Nixon Administration announced a new nuclear strategy in National Security Decision Memorandum 242, the United States has officially pursued the second of these two alternatives.[16] By providing the President with more options than either mutual annihilation or surrender in a nuclear crisis, these "limited nuclear option" (LNO) strategies attempt to control the escalation of the conflict. By attempting to limit the conflict as it progresses, and striving to maintain command, control, communication, and intelligence linkages in wartime, some of these LNO strategies strive for the United States to "survive" or "prevail" in a protracted nuclear conflict.

The Reagan Administration did not modify this official strategic policy substantially, but the language used by administration officials to justify the policy changed rather dramatically. What Carter Administration officials referred to, in Presidential Directive 59, as targeting and escalatory "options," became "nuclear warfighting" to Caspar Weinberger.[17] A confidential Department of Defense memorandum leaked to the press in May, 1982 stated: "the accrued forces are ordered to prepare for nuclear counterattacks against the Soviet Union over a protracted period" and "must prevail and be able to force the Soviet Union to seek earliest termination of hostilities on terms favorable to the United States."[18] Statements such as these aroused alarm among many Americans, even though the policies being described were not really new. This rhetorical stance perhaps contributed to antinuclear sentiment in the United States.

Loose Defense Department talk about limited nuclear war was accompanied by proposals for a massive civil defense plan for the United States. Cities throughout the nation were provided with extensive relocation plans, and were asked to provide support for the federal government in ensuring the smooth implementation of such plans in the event of a nuclear attack against the United States.[19] The national debate over civil defense was not new, of course, given the federal government's attempts in the 1950s and '60s to encourage Americans to build fallout shelters and develop evacuation plans.[20] These earlier attempts suffered the same fate as the Reagan Administration's efforts to establish a national civil defense plan. After stimulating a vigorous national debate over the wisdom and feasibility of civil defense, most Americans in the 1950s, 1960s, and 1980s concluded that attempts to survive an all-out nuclear war were futile.[21]

The importance of Reagan's civil defense proposal for nuclear freeze organizers, however, was that it called for local governments to consider the plans, debate them, and take action. The result was to bring the whole issue of nuclear war and its effects down to the local level. As city councils studied and considered these plans, public information about the destructive effects of nuclear weapons proliferated. This knowledge was to become a major factor contributing to public support of the nuclear freeze campaign.[22] City councils all over the nation began to reject the administration's relocation plans as unworkable and as potentially dangerous parts in a strategy to fight and win a protracted nuclear war.[23]

Administration officials not only talked about potentially surviving a limited nuclear war, and urged localities to adopt civil defense plans in the event of such a war, but also adopted an increasingly belligerent rhetorical posture toward the Soviet Union. During Reagan's first term in office, Soviet-American relations reached their lowest point in decades.[24] Hostile language about the Soviet "evil empire," combined with official silence about the nuclear arms control negotiations, only magnified the public's fear of nuclear war. These increasing concerns about the nuclear arms race were reflected in public opinion polls. A January, 1983 Louis Harris poll found that sixty-six percent of those surveyed believed that Reagan was doing an unsatisfactory job in arms control, and fifty-seven percent were worried that he might get the United States involved in a nuclear war.[25] The rhetorical stance of the Reagan Administration early in its first term undoubtedly moved many Americans to ask whether the United States actually was preparing to fight and win a nuclear war against its primary adversary. This fear proved to be fertile ground for the grassroots nuclear freeze campaign.

The nuclear freeze proposal itself was born before Reagan took office. In 1980, Randall Forsberg, founder of the Institute for Defense and Disarmament Studies in Brookline, Massachusetts, wrote "A Call to Halt the Nuclear Arms Race: Proposal for a Mutual U. S.–Soviet Nuclear Weapons Freeze," in an attempt to formulate an arms control proposal that could capture the imaginations of the public and arms control specialists alike. In the proposal, Forsberg called for a mutual freeze on the testing, production, and deployment of nuclear weapons and delivery systems. She focused on the new danger posed by highly accurate counterforce weapons, claiming that this new generation of weapons under development would be destabilizing in a time of crisis. She argued that the proposal could be verified through national technical means currently available and through the cooperation of the International Atomic Energy Agency. She claimed that freezing the arms race would preserve the existing parity between the two nuclear superpowers, and that the economies of both nations would benefit. She concluded by suggesting that the freeze would be only the first step towards gradual reductions in nuclear arsenals, culminating eventually in general nuclear disarmament.

Activists in New England got word of Forsberg's proposal, and began to develop a strategy for arousing local support for the freeze. These early organizers were committed to a decentralized, community approach to political action, and their efforts on behalf of the nuclear freeze proposal reflected this belief. Coffee meetings in individual homes, neighborhood discussion sessions, local city council debates, and local referenda became the hallmarks of the nuclear freeze campaign.[26] As word spread, more and more localities in New England adopted resolutions in support of the freeze proposal. Soon the freeze campaign caught the attention of activists nationwide. By the end of 1981, over 45,000 organizers were working actively to promote the nuclear freeze in their localities.[27] In March, 1981, freeze supporters held their first national conference, during which a National Clearinghouse was established in St. Louis, Missouri, to provide information and guidance to any local citizen interested in promoting the nuclear freeze.

As the freeze proposal gained supporters nationwide, it began to appear on state referenda. Well-organized campaigns appeared, including fundraising efforts, direct mail strategies, and advertising campaigns. The freeze proposal entered national politics on March 10, 1982, when it was introduced into Congress in the form of a Joint Resolution, with bipartisan sponsorship. Democrat Edward Kennedy and Republican Mark Hatfield introduced the resolution into the Senate, while Congressmen Ed Markey, Silvio Conte, and Jonathan Bingham introduced it into the House of Representatives.[28] What began as a localized, grassroots effort to educate citizens about the arms race had evolved into a significant political call that national legislators could not ignore.

While the freeze resolution was debated fiercely in Congress, public support for the idea of a nuclear weapons moratorium grew dramatically. A Louis Harris poll, conducted in late 1982, revealed that seventy-six percent of those surveyed supported the idea of a nuclear freeze. Eighty-five percent of the same sample, however, believed that the Soviet Union was a hostile power, and fifty-one percent, the highest percentage since the late 1950s, believed that the Soviets were an outright enemy of the United States.[29] Most Americans supported the concept of a nuclear freeze, but only if it was bilateral and would not result in a significant Soviet military advantage. These hesitations surrounding the nuclear freeze proposal were not evident in the largest political rally in American history, when 750,000 citizens gathered in New York City to call for an end to the nuclear arms race and the adoption of a nuclear freeze.[30]

To understand the broad public support for the proposal to freeze the arms race, it is helpful to examine the discourse of nuclear freeze advocates. An examination of the published discourse of some of the most vocal and visible advocates of the proposal reveals five main themes that constituted the core rhetoric of the campaign: (1) faith in common sense; (2) fear of nuclear war; (3) concern about nuclear overkill; (4) a sense of urgency; and

(5) impatience with traditional arms control. These five themes interpene-
trated one another in ways that created a sense of concern and empowerment among freeze supporters. Although compelling to a fearful public,
these themes created some rhetorical difficulties for the campaign when
challenged by the discourse of the Reagan Administration.

The Rhetoric of the Nuclear Freeze

In "A Dramatistic Theory of the Rhetoric of Movements," Leland Griffin
eloquently described in Burkean terms the rhetorical stages through which
social movements progress.[31] Initially, symbolic order is preserved, as
humans strive to maintain the existing structure and hierarchy of meaning. But as the symbolic order gradually fails to preserve unity through
communion and identification, and becomes increasingly unjust in the
eyes of the alienated, rival sects begin to form to challenge the existing
order. As Griffin argued:

> And thus, perversely goaded by the spirit of hierarchy, moved by
> the impious dream of a mythic new Order...they are moved to
> Act: moved, ingenious men ("inventors of the negative") to rise
> up and cry No to the existing order—and prophesy the coming
> of the new. And thus movements begin.[32]

The nuclear freeze campaign rose up and loudly shouted No: No to traditional arms control experts; No to nuclear war; No to new counterforce-
capable weapons. They prophesied a new Order: one free of the fear of
atomic warfare; one characterized by nuclear disarmament; one that
involved ordinary citizens in life and death decisions. These themes are
illustrated in the discourse of nuclear freeze advocates.

Faith in Common Sense

The first theme found in pro-freeze rhetoric, faith in common sense, justified giving the common person a voice in the debate over the deployment
and potential use of nuclear weapons. The simplicity of the proposal itself,
referred to by some opponents as "bumper sticker arms control," meant

that it was easily accessible to ordinary citizens who were concerned, but not necessarily technically informed, about nuclear weapons strategy.[33] Father Robert Drinan argued, for example, that the nuclear freeze was "the clearest, simplest proposal ever made by non-professional defense specialists to do something concrete."[34]

Contrasted with the formidable complexity of traditional arms control proposals, the nuclear freeze was attractive, Bernard Feld argued, because it embodied "an obvious and basic fact of nature," that if people wish to reverse the direction in which they are traveling, they first must stop; only then is it possible to change direction.[35] Another freeze advocate, Jack Mendelsohn, argued that the proposal "identifies and celebrates fundamental, graspable, irrefutable principles of human experience," namely that it is impossible to increase and decrease something at the same time, and, thus, that the United States must first stop the arms race before it can reduce nuclear arsenals.[36] Randy Kehler, the national coordinator for the freeze, contended that "because the bilateral freeze is so inherently clear and comprehensible, because it makes so much common sense, it is winning the support of a wide spectrum of American people."[37]

The nuclear freeze proposal appealed to the common sense of ordinary citizens because it gave voice to a very human response towards the nuclear threat; emotion. Father Drinan claimed that the freeze was a "*cri de coeur*" rather than a program from the mind, while commentator Mary Ellen Leary embraced this "primitive clamor for humanity's survival, which may be the only response adequate to the apocalyptic threat."[38] Republican Senator Mark Hatfield, who co-sponsored the Joint Resolution in the Senate, explicitly embraced the power and authority of emotion when he argued: "There are those who caution against this departure from the norm. They admonish us to proceed slowly, and implore us to think logically. Look where our so-called caution and logic have taken us."[39]

The common sense approach to arms control embodied in the freeze not only acknowledged the emotional aspects of the nuclear arms race but, in fact, celebrated them. By attempting to regain public control over an issue that had been left to the detached rationality of experts, the freeze represented a "democratization" of the issue of nuclear war.[40] In the introduction to their book, *Freeze! How You Can Help Prevent Nuclear War*,

Senators Edward Kennedy and Mark Hatfield argued that the freeze was "a clear and compelling call which any citizen can read and which every citizen can answer."[41]

Faith in common sense was perhaps the campaign's most powerful discursive theme. Individual citizens, who were concerned and affected by this momentous issue, were called to challenge the authority of nuclear experts and express their heart-felt beliefs that the arms race must stop. An appeal to common sense empowered individual citizens, and reassured them that they could understand complex problems and contribute to finding solutions. Given its grounding in "common sense" principles, its attempt to recapture individual human agency and its embrace of emotion, this type of discourse could reach out and appeal to a wide public audience.

Fear of Nuclear War

Another theme that emerges in the rhetoric of the nuclear freeze advocates, and one that is related to the notion of common sense, is that a full-scale nuclear war between the United States and the Soviet Union would be a tragedy beyond all conceivable proportions. As I argued earlier, the public's fear of nuclear war was fueled by official discussions of limited nuclear wars, civil defense evacuation plans, and the "evil empire." At the same time, however, an organization called Physicians for Social Responsibility, led by Harvard pediatrician Helen Caldicott, was warning the public about the medical consequences of nuclear war. Caldicott vociferously attacked the "madness" of the nuclear arms race in a national speaking tour, where she painted a very vivid picture of what life would be like in American cities following a nuclear attack.[42] In an address at the American Humanist Association's National Conference in 1982, Caldicott described what would happen if a nuclear bomb exploded at that moment:

> Dropped at ground level, it will burn with the heat of the sun and dig a hole three-quarters of a mile wide and eight hundred feet deep, converting all the buildings, all of us, and the earth below to radioactive fallout.... Out to a radius of six miles from here, every person would be killed, many actually vaporized. We could never do that before nuclear weapons—vaporize people. Most of

the body is water and, when exposed to the heat of the sun, we just turn into gas. We've already done it—there are pictures and photographs of shadows of people from Hiroshima.[43]

She continued her grisly description by explaining the firestorms, famines, and plagues that would likely follow an all-out nuclear exchange.[44]

Other antinuclear advocates joined Caldicott in describing for the public what it would be like to experience a nuclear war. Jonathan Schell's popular book, *The Fate of the Earth*, devoted ninety-six pages to an excruciatingly detailed account of the horrible effects of nuclear explosions.[45] A 1983 made-for-television movie called *The Day After* visually portrayed a nuclear attack from the vantage point of residents of Lawrence, Kansas. Kennedy and Hatfield's book contained maps and charts delineating the location and numbers of casualties in hundreds of American cities in the event of nuclear war.[46] These ghastly descriptions of nuclear annihilation attempted to induce readers and viewers to visualize the effects of nuclear war, so that they could imagine it on an individual level, and hopefully be shocked into action against the arms race.[47]

Although some argued that such "apocalyptic pornography" was inaccurate, and only intensified public fear and paralysis, it is quite clear that these fear appeals were designed to motivate the public into activism.[48] Nuclear freeze advocates wanted to shake up their audience's sense of complacency through fear appeals. Whether this strategy succeeded in generating support for the freeze or merely frightened listeners into fatalism and apathy is unclear. But when descriptions of these gruesome details were combined with appeals to common sense, pro-freeze discourse attempted to convince citizens that, although the nuclear issue is daunting and difficult to think about, ordinary people could contribute to preventing nuclear war. The central message of the freeze was that Americans did not need to trust experts to remove their fears. In this sense, pro-freeze rhetoric offered at least a glimmer of hope for its adherents.

Concern About Nuclear Overkill

Related to the theme of fear, advocates of the nuclear freeze claimed that the United States and the Soviet Union possessed more than enough nuclear weapons in their attempts to establish a stable deterrent posture. This "nuclear overkill" theme was not new to the peace movement. As early as 1963, some argued that America's nuclear arsenal was too large, and that much lower levels of armament would suffice to deter attacks against the United States.[49] By 1983, however, the superpowers' nuclear arsenals were swollen to the point that they contained the equivalent of 6,000 pounds of TNT for every man, woman, and child on the planet.[50] After describing in detail the devastation in Hiroshima and Nagasaki, Senators Kennedy and Hatfield wrote, "The overkill is obvious.... [E]ach side has enough strategic nuclear weapons in its stockpile to inflict hundreds of thousands of Hiroshimas on the other."[51] Caldicott argued that the "little boys" in the Pentagon and the Kremlin had

> thirty thousand nuclear weapons. *Thirty thousand....* But that's not enough. The Reagan Administration wants seventeen thousand more intercontinental missiles in the next ten years. *Seventeen thousand!* Can you even contemplate how many that is? How long does it take you to count up to a thousand? There are only about one thousand cities in the Soviet Union.[52]

One implication of this discourse is not *necessarily* that the superpowers must renounce nuclear weapons altogether, but rather that the arms race has accelerated to such an absurd degree that the entire planet could be destroyed if the weapons were detonated. As Jack Mendelsohn aptly put it, "enough is enough."[53]

By denouncing the overkill present in U. S. strategic arsenals, nuclear freeze advocates could reject the acceleration of the arms race and advocate a situation of minimal deterrence. Although complete nuclear disarmament was the ultimate goal of many campaign leaders, the freeze proposal itself did not envision drastic unilateral measures. Given the apparent public fear of the Soviet Union's military might, this aspect of pro-freeze rhetoric was especially important. To be successful in challenging Reagan's nuclear buildup, freeze advocates had to be careful to avoid embracing proposals that appeared to weaken the U. S. relative to the U. S. S. R. The administration somehow would have to portray the freeze as dangerous to American national security, if it was successfully to diffuse the freeze campaign.

A Sense of Urgency

Another important theme in pro-freeze discourse was the claim that the time available to stop the arms race was running out. Advocates claimed that the freeze had to be adopted soon or the chances for ending the arms race would come to an end. They established the timeliness of the proposal by arguing that new destabilizing weapons systems were on the verge of being developed and deployed. If these highly accurate counterforce weapons, such as the MX and Trident II missiles, were deployed, advocates claimed that stable, strategic parity would be destroyed.

Freeze proponents contended that the superpowers' arsenals were, at that time, basically at equal levels. Hatfield cited statements by the Joint Chiefs of Staff, who claimed that they would not be willing to trade America's nuclear arsenal for that of the Soviet Union.[54] If a freeze were adopted immediately, therefore, this state of strategic stability could be preserved.[55] The accuracy of proposed new weapons systems, however, would make them destabilizing in a crisis, in that the adversary would be forced to adopt a hairtrigger launch on warning policy in order to attempt to preserve its retaliatory nuclear forces.[56] Kennedy and Hatfield explicitly drew a distinction between existing nuclear forces and the new systems when they argued, "[A]nd it is that new arms race, not the present situation, which could irrevocably shatter the present balance."[57]

George Ball, Under Secretary of State in the Johnson Administration, pointed out the importance of acting in a timely manner on the freeze proposal, when he stated: "The Kennedy-Hatfield Resolution provides a sensible alternative to continuing the arms race to the point where the advent of increasingly complex and elaborate new weapons systems will close off *our last clear chance* for effective negotiation"[58] (My emphasis). The sense of urgency underlying the freeze was put most forcefully by Hatfield, when he claimed:

> If there was ever a time to be bold—this is it. If there was ever a time to abandon political considerations—this is the moment. If there was ever a time to reject the misleading "strangelovian" terminology in which we all indulge for the sake of appearing serious—this is the time.[59]

Creating a sense of urgency was necessary if the freeze campaign was to achieve public support quickly and dramatically. Urgency, combined with common sense and fear, necessitated quick action, and the freeze campaign did indeed rapidly spread and gain supporters nationwide. In 1982, after only one year of active organizational efforts, the freeze was the subject of debate in the U. S. Congress. This rapid buildup of public support was fueled by the sense of urgency embodied in pro-freeze rhetoric.

Impatience with Traditional Arms Control

Calls for quick adoption of a nuclear moratorium stands in sharp contrast to the slow, deliberate, and often painstaking efforts of traditional arms control negotiators. Years of difficult negotiations were required before the SALT I, SALT II, and INF treaties were ready for signatures, and the advocates of a nuclear freeze voiced their impatience with this process. Some freeze supporters claimed that arms control in the past served simply to manage and fine tune the arms race, not to slow it down.[60] Christopher Paine went even further, claiming that the arms control community acquiesced to the national security establishment. He argued:

> the dominant conventional wisdom in arms control is becoming the tangled product of an ongoing and debilitating Faustian bargain with the national security establishment. At the risk of over-simplification, let me nevertheless characterize this bargain as follows: it appears to have sought "stability" in the strategic military relationship by establishing limitations on strategic offensive nuclear weapons.... The price paid for getting the powers-that-be to entertain such notions was, and continues to be, passive acquiescence in the very doctrines, strategies, and nuclear forces for "extended deterrence" which are driving the arms race forward, thereby guaranteeing that arms control has become an exercise in *managing* rather than *ending* the nuclear arms race.[61]

The nuclear freeze proposal was an attempt to cut through the highly technical, doctrinaire logic of the arms control community in order to achieve actual reductions in the nuclear arsenals of the superpowers. As Kennedy claimed, the freeze was an attempt to make arms control "more than just rulemaking for a barely controlled arms race."[62] By emphasizing that the freeze proposal was merely a first step, creating a stable strategic and symbolic environment conducive to productive negotiations for actual disarmament, advocates proposed to go beyond the immobility of traditional arms control techniques.

Common sense, fear, concern about nuclear overkill, a feeling of urgency, and impatience with arms control, combined to provide a powerful rhetorical challenge to the Reagan Administration's nuclear policies. Kennedy and Hatfield effectively unified these themes into a concluding plea for the freeze:

> It is time, perhaps the last period of time we shall have, to cease debating the preferred options of certain experts and public figures who think that there is a better way to dot the i's or cross the t's of arms control. The freeze concept has the inestimable political virtues of simplicity and practicality. Its benefits to humanity are readily apparent to ordinary human beings, rather than to only a select handful of scientists and strategic analysts. There would be no mistaking the moral implications of an agreement to stop the arms race now, and an intense national and international campaign for ratification could be effectively mounted. To a world increasingly apprehensive over the awesome dangers and technological complexities of the arms race, a freeze offers the symbol and the substance of hope.[63]

The political and symbolic challenge that the freeze campaign posed to the administration was by no means a weak one. Average Americans lost faith in the established structure of meaning and chose to challenge it. They proclaimed an alternative that offered hope for a future liberated from the fear and confusion of the present. These voices were not alone, however; they were joined by the institutions of established religion, which became deeply involved in the debate over nuclear weapons policy. The religious community's debate over the arms race is worth examining, given its emphasis on the moral issues surrounding nuclear weapons and its involvement in the public debate.

The Antinuclear Rhetoric of Organized Religion

Catholic, Protestant, and Jewish groups in the United States were actively involved in the antinuclear activism of the early 1980s. Robert Spaeth argued that the religious community in America became more willing to speak out against nuclear weapons as the issue gained public attention. This willingness spawned a great debate over the morality of the arms race.[64] American policy requires moral backing, if it is to be congruent with the nation's self-image of high moral purpose. Administration speaker Eugene Rostow stated, "if our government's policies ultimately are to succeed, then these policies must be on a sound moral basis."[65] At a minimum, if administration policy is publicly rejected as immoral and unjust by religious institutions, it is more vulnerable to partisan political attack than if it is accepted and embraced as morally sound. The religious debate over nuclear weapons, therefore, is important to examine when considering governmental reactions to the nuclear freeze campaign.

Religious organizations were involved in promoting the nuclear freeze through public education in the church and by actively endorsing and participating in the campaign itself. Organizations such as Pax Christi, Clergy and Laity Concerned, the American Friends Service Committee, and the Fellowship of Reconciliation were all active supporters of the nuclear freeze. In fact, one-third of American Catholic bishops claim to have been actively involved in the peace movement.[66]

During 1982, many churches officially endorsed the nuclear weapons freeze proposal through their respective hierarchies. The United Methodist Church, the Christian Church (Disciples of Christ), the General Assembly of the United Presbyterian Church in the U. S. A., the Lutheran Church in America, and the Union of Hebrew Congregations, to name a few, publicly stated their support for a freeze.[67] But the most fascinating, and perhaps the most influential, internal church debate involved the National Council of Catholic Bishops' attempts to formulate a comprehensive and detailed moral examination of the nuclear arms race in a pastoral letter entitled, "The Challenge of Peace: God's Promise and Our Response." In preparing the document, the Bishops consulted advisors of varying political persuasions and carefully examined nuclear weapons systems, doctrines, and potential explosive effects.[68] The most controversial portions of the document concerned the morality of different aspects of nuclear strategy; the actual use of nuclear weapons, counterforce targeting, and nuclear deterrence.

The Bishops called upon theological consensus to support their claim that it is categorically immoral to use nuclear weapons against civilian populations, even in retaliatory strikes.[69] Such an action clearly would violate well-established "just war" requirements concerning proportionality and discrimination between combatants and noncombatants. Similarly, the Bishops rejected counterforce targeting, claiming that the use of even the most limited and accurate weapons would most likely escalate into all-out war. They concluded that the risk of such rapid escalation overrode the potential military benefits that might be accrued by such an attack.[70] Even if counterforce attacks could be controlled and limited, they still would fail to meet the just war criterion of discrimination, since the current United States targeting plan includes sixty "military" targets in Moscow alone and 40,000 nationwide.[71] The Bishops argued that the unintended civilian casualties in such a limited counterforce attack would be morally intolerable.

If the use of nuclear weapons is immoral, regardless of how they are targeted, then, an obvious question to be raised is whether it is morally acceptable to even possess nuclear weapons. The Bishops considered the morality of nuclear deterrence by questioning whether it is moral to intend to do what is immoral to actually carry out. In other words, is it morally acceptable for the United States government to intend to annihilate the Soviet Union, even if it never actually carries out its intention? In ethical terms, this question is very complex. For example, consider the question of intent. What is the intent of nuclear deterrence? Does the United States intend to annihilate Soviet citizens or to prevent their annihilation? The ultimate purpose of nuclear deterrence is to prevent war, not make it more likely. But to make the system of deterrence work, the United States realistically and actually must intend to carry out that threat of annihilation. If the threat is not believable, then the system breaks down.

Some claim that this ambiguity in determining the "actual" intent of deterrence renders it morally tolerable as a stopgap measure.[72] Others claim that the intent of the policy can be determined by its consequences; if a new weapons system actually does stabilize the nuclear balance, then the intent of its deployment is to prevent war. If not, the intent is annihilation, and the weapons system is morally intolerable.[73] Still others claim that the ends do not justify the means; in other words, the immorality of the instrumental intention (annihilation) is not superceded by the morality of the consummatory intention (prevention of war.)[74]

Given this complex controversy, the Catholic Bishops were faced with a difficult choice in deciding the morality of nuclear deterrence. Although the first draft of the pastoral letter pronounced nuclear deterrence immoral, the final draft concluded that it is morally tolerable, but only as a step on the way to general nuclear disarmament.[75] Even with this lukewarm endorsement, the Catholic Bishops' pastoral letter was an unequivocal rejection of the nuclear arms race. With the institutional hierarchy, symbolic power, and organizational efforts of the Catholic Church behind them, the Bishops posed a serious challenge to Reagan's nuclear arms buildup.

The Vulnerability of Antinuclear Discourse

Given the strong public support for the nuclear freeze proposal in the early years of the Reagan Administration, estimated at seventy percent in March, 1982, one could conclude that support for Reagan's policies was diminishing.[76] It would be misleading to suggest, however, that the symbolic appeal of Reagan's campaign call to make America strong again had disappeared completely. The mythic new symbolic order envisioned by nuclear freeze supporters, though challenging to the old one, suffered from the same fatal flaw as all other human symbolic acts: it fell short of perfection. A closer examination of the rhetorical themes of freeze advocates and the religious community, in fact, reveals at least three potential ways in which Reagan could debunk the appeal of the freeze proposal and firmly establish a rhetorical base for the Strategic Defense Initiative.

First, the most obvious difficulty with the rhetoric of the freeze proposal, from the perspective of the Reagan Administration, was its failure to adequately assess and respond to the Soviet threat. The same Louis Harris poll which reported public support for the nuclear freeze at seventy-six percent also revealed the public's fear of the Soviet Union. Eighty-five percent of those polled believed the Soviets were a hostile power, and fifty-one percent believed they were an outright enemy of the United

States.[77] Pro-freeze discourse, however, only seemed to focus on American weapons systems—the MX, B-1, and Trident II. Rarely did freeze activists base their appeals upon the awesome danger posed by a new generation of accurate Soviet weapons systems.

Although Kennedy briefly discussed the Soviet threat, he concluded that mutual interests in survival transcended any political or ideological differences. He argued that America should not enter into a mutual freeze "because we like the Soviets or they like us," but because both nations preferred survival to extinction.[78] Similarly, religious documents opposing the arms race paid little attention to the immorality of Soviet tyranny and, when they did so, most concluded that ending the arms race was more important than ideological or national differences.[79]

These passing references to the Soviet Union's military might did not satisfy those skeptical of the wisdom of adopting a nuclear freeze. The Reagan Administration took advantage of this aspect of the freeze proposal, arguing that the idea was perhaps well-intentioned but misguided and dangerous. Opponents of the freeze argued that its adoption would lock the United States into a position of strategic inferiority, thus leaving the nation dangerously unprotected. Arguing that the Soviet arsenal was numerically superior in throw weight, missile warheads, ICBMs, SLBMs, and bombers, administration speakers claimed that adopting a freeze prior to the completion of the Reagan arms buildup would give the Soviets a permanent military advantage.[80] Even worse, they claimed, a freeze would prevent Reagan's strategic modernization program from proceeding, thereby providing no solution to ICBM vulnerability and no replacement for the aging B-52 fleet.[81] Even in a situation of nuclear overkill, if one accepts the assumptions that the Soviet threat is real and that its leaders take advantage of weakness, these vulnerabilities in the U. S. nuclear arsenal are important. If a freeze would lock America into a position of strategic inferiority, the nation's doom would be sealed, given the inadequacy of the current deterrent posture.

The administration's focus on the Soviet threat as an argument against the nuclear freeze proposal was probably an effective strategy, given the public's attitude towards the Kremlin. It was quite clear that the average American citizen in 1982 was fearful of the Soviet Union. But the average American was also afraid of the dangers inherent in the escalating nuclear arms race. Neither a massive military buildup nor a nuclear freeze alone would serve to soothe both of these fears simultaneously. An advanced ballistic missile defense system, however, like the Strategic Defense Initiative, would perhaps so serve. If technologically feasible, such a system would protect the American homeland from nuclear devastation in the event of war, while allowing the continuation of a nuclear buildup to counter the Soviet military threat. In this way, SDI could be seen as a more comprehensive solution to public uncertainty and fear than either a nuclear freeze or a buildup.

The second difficulty with the rhetoric of nuclear freeze advocates concerned their treatment of the issue of nuclear deterrence. Freeze advocates and the Catholic Bishops accepted the viability of deterrence, at least until the long-term goal of nuclear disarmament was achieved. This acceptance of deterrence was evident in their claim that the freeze should be adopted immediately, since the U. S. and Soviet forces were relatively equal in size. The assumption of this claim is that strategic parity deters war; only destabilizing counterforce weapons can trigger the holocaust. The freeze advocates' denunciation of nuclear overkill also reveals this underlying acceptance of nuclear deterrence, since the argument assumes that only a few nuclear weapons are needed to deter war.

Accepting nuclear deterrence, however, created rhetorical difficulties for antinuclear activists. The horrifying reality of holding innocent civilians hostage to nuclear annihilation in order to reduce the chances that war will occur does not adequately soothe the public's fear of nuclear weapons. Once one is educated about nuclear weapons and aroused into taking political action against continued deployment, the tenuous peace that exists under the shadow of the bomb does not feel like true peace at all. Unless freeze advocates could successfully persuade their supporters that disarmament was a realistic long term outcome of a nuclear freeze process, their solution to the arms race seemed rather bittersweet.

Reagan's SDI program offered the hope of breaking out of the madness of holding nuclear hostages altogether. By promising a future characterized by mutually assured survival, rather than mutually assured destruction, the vision of SDI would seem to be much more appealing to a public fearful of nuclear weapons than even a nuclear freeze and gradual disarmament. In addition, by imposing a seemingly simple, although technologically complex solution upon the difficult moral questions of nuclear deterrence, Reagan apparently proposed a more moral solution to the arms race than even the American Catholic Bishops. If SDI could eliminate the need for nuclear deterrence, then it was both safer and more morally sound than a nuclear freeze.

The third potential difficulty with the rhetorical themes of the nuclear freeze campaign concerned its attitude toward experts and technology. The freeze proposal itself was grounded in a skeptical, even negative, view of nuclear experts. The most unique aspect of the campaign and its discourse was its faith in the common sense of ordinary citizens to decide this issue. The grassroots approach of the organizers empowered individual citizens to take part in public discussions about nuclear war. Educational campaigns intended to inform people about nuclear weapons, hardware, doctrine, and strategy were an integral part of the movement. Technological solutions to insecurity, embodied in the new generation of accurate nuclear delivery systems, were rejected outright by nuclear freeze supporters as additions, not solutions, to insecurity. The religious community, although passionately defending their right to judge the morality of this political and technological dilemma, conceded that their expertise lay only in the moral arena, not the technical. The Catholic Bishops explicitly admitted that it was not their place to comment on technical matters, only on the morality of the principles involved.[82]

The freeze campaign's rejection of technology created an opportunity for Reagan to do what he did best: express optimism and faith in the American way of life. Saying No to the inexorable march of technology, progress, American ingenuity, and optimism is difficult to sustain, given America's self-image as a moral and progressive nation with new frontiers to conquer. Improvement, advancement, refinement, and progress are deeply embedded in the American sociopolitical consciousness. The symbolic structure of Reagan's SDI program tapped into these values, and, in fact, directed them toward developing a solution to the most dire dilemma the world has ever faced. The stakes, therefore, were ultimate, and Reagan's SDI discourse urged Americans to rely on their optimism and faith in this nation to help find a solution to the nuclear arms race that could be counted on: a technological solution.

In summary, the resurgence of public awareness and activism concerning nuclear weapons policies in the early 1980s created significant controversy, and provided a direct challenge to the Reagan Administration's attempts to modernize and expand America's nuclear arsenal. The nuclear weapons freeze debate and the pronouncements of the religious community demanded and called forth a response from the administration. Reagan's proposal to pursue the Strategic Defense Initiative can be viewed as one such response. In the next chapter, I explore the symbolic appeal of this controversial project through an analysis of the Reagan Administration's pro-SDI discourse. The weaknesses and vulnerabilities of the rhetoric of the nuclear freeze campaign become more apparent when viewed from the perspective of an idealistic vision of ballistic missile defense.

4.
The Symbolic Power of SDI

ON MARCH 23, 1983, President Ronald Reagan addressed the nation on prime time television to discuss issues of national security and defense. Near the end of the address, Reagan called for a program of research into technologies that potentially could intercept and destroy incoming ballistic missiles before they reached their targets. Reagan asked his listeners:

> What if free people could live secure in the knowledge that their security did not rest upon the threat of instant U. S. retaliation to deter a Soviet attack, that we could intercept and destroy strategic ballistic missiles before they reached our own soil or that of our allies?[1]

The speech went on to outline the Strategic Defense Initiative, a controversial project designed to explore the technical feasibility of ballistic missile defenses. The purpose of this chapter is to analyze the Reagan Administration's SDI discourse, derived from transcripts of speeches, news conferences, press releases, and congressional testimony, in order to explain its symbolic appeal.[2]

I shall argue that the rhetorical stance adopted by the Reagan Administration in its defense of SDI was symbolically powerful and difficult for opponents to challenge. First, Reagan's call for research into ballistic missile defense technologies appealed to the nation's historical sense of mission and destiny, as outlined in chapter 2. The new frontiers of outer space and scientific advancement were to be conquered by the SDI project, just as the old frontiers of the western United States were conquered by American pioneers. In addition, as a "nonaggressive, defensive" weapon system, SDI appealed to the nation's perceived morality and innocence in foreign

65

affairs, which is grounded in various symbolic constructions and interpretations of United States history.

Second, SDI effectively captured the symbolic appeal of the nuclear freeze proposal and nuclear disarmament, as outlined in chapter 3. Touted as a way to make nuclear weapons virtually obsolete, SDI sought to free Americans from the paralyzing fear of nuclear war. At the same time, however, SDI seemed less risky than nuclear disarmament, in that it served as a hedge against Soviet violations of disarmament agreements, nuclear accidents, terrorism, and nuclear proliferation.

Third, on a deeper symbolic level, Reagan's SDI rhetoric reflected and reinforced humanity's desire to escape from the negative implications of language and symbol use and return to a pre-nuclear, pre-symbolic innocence. But, as I will demonstrate, Reagan's solution to the arms race, as embodied in SDI, only leads to an illusion of innocence, as well as an illusion of transcendence above material conditions. On the contrary, SDI represents a complete surrender to the realm of non-symbolic motion, with the attendant loss of freedom implied by such a move.

Fourth, Reagan's SDI discourse created a situation whereby the program was insulated from strong criticism, and simultaneously, was rhetorically self-perpetuating. Given that SDI was justified primarily as a research program designed to explore the feasibility of emerging technologies, it was difficult for opponents to formulate compelling arguments against it. Arguments challenging the design of the system, and its probable cost and effectiveness, were dismissed with calls for further research, and, since these uncertainties could only be resolved with more research, SDI became self-perpetuating.

Before developing these conclusions in more detail, a brief description of Reagan's March 23, 1983 speech is necessary, because it set the stage for future debate over SDI by defining the nature of the program and its purposes. In this way, the speech served to shape and constrain the pro-SDI discourse that was to follow.

Reagan's "Star Wars" Address

Reagan introduced his SDI program only after engaging in a plea for public and congressional support for his offensive nuclear strategic modernization programs. In the early part of the speech, where Reagan described the state of the nation's defenses and the growing Soviet threat, he emphasized the "scene." Kenneth Burke argued that discourse featuring the pentadic element of scene corresponds to a philosophy of materialism. When considerations of scene are dominant, the discourse implies that the realm of human *action* in some way has been reduced to *motion.*[3] Burke's distinction between action and motion is important to my argument. He claimed that action involves choice, which implies the human ability to evaluate a situation and then decide upon an "appropriate" response to that situation. Language use is action for Burke, in that humans strategically "name" situations to accomplish certain purposes. Motion, on the other hand, is outside the realm of symbol use; it involves physical movement that occurs without the intervention of human motives or actions. Discourse such as Reagan's, in this situation, metaphorically implies that such events (the scene) are driving history, and that they are frighteningly beyond human control. Humans have lost control over their destiny, and are subject to the whim of nature. Free will has been surrendered to materialistic determinism, as human agents are caught in a scene over which they have no control. Reagan, in describing the nuclear arms race and the Soviet threat, described such a scene, and explained how it was dangerous and menacing.

The scene described by Reagan was one of despair and hopelessness due to the dependence on mutual assured destruction to keep the peace. Reagan claimed that reliance on "the specter of retaliation, on mutual threat" was "a sad commentary on the human condition."[4] Even though MAD kept the peace for more than three decades, he argued, it created a situation of perpetual fear and despair. By focusing on the ever-present shadow of the nuclear arms race, Reagan portrayed a dismal and hopeless scene from which there seemed to be no escape. In this drama human agents are constrained by the scene; the arms race seems to have a life of its own. Humanity can find no way out of the nuclear dilemma.

The scene is threatening not only due to the material existence of nuclear weapons, but also due to a menacing agent present in the scene: the Soviet Union. Reagan claimed that the world situation, characterized by a dangerous Soviet offensive buildup, instability in Third World nations, and calls for defense budget cuts in the Congress, led to an extremely threatening situation, one that risked the very existence of American institutions and values. He depicted the Soviet threat in these terms:

> For 20 years the Soviet Union has been accumulating enormous military might. They didn't stop when their forces exceeded all requirements of a legitimate defensive capability. And they haven't stopped now. During the past decade and a half, the Soviets have built up a massive arsenal of new strategic nuclear weapons—weapons that can strike directly at the United States.[5]

This massive Soviet buildup, according to Reagan, unfortunately occurred at the same time that Democratic members of Congress were slashing the defense budget. As a result, Reagan warned, the scene was as dangerous as that of the 1930s, when the democracies who neglected their defenses "invited the tragedy of World War II." He argued that "We must not let that grim chapter of history repeat itself through apathy or neglect."[6] In this way, the physical threat represented by nuclear weapons is magnified by the presence of an enemy armed with such weapons. In this scene, as Reagan described it, Americans would naturally feel fearful and helpless.

Toward the end of his address, however, the focus of Reagan's speech shifted from "scene" to "purpose." Burke contended that discourse featuring the pentadic element of purpose corresponds with a philosophy of mysticism. When purpose is dominant in a symbolic act, the discourse attempts to identify the audience with the ultimate ground of existence, or some universal concept of being. An element of unity and oneness is prominent, as the discourse develops "an ideal of passive contemplation" in which individuals transcend differences and achieve utter union with one another.[7]

In proposing SDI, Reagan offered "a vision of the future which offers hope. It is that we embark on a program to counter the awesome Soviet missile threat with measures that are defensive."[8] In proposing SDI, Reagan claimed that his "only purpose—one all people share—is to search for ways to reduce the danger of nuclear war."[9] This was a purpose that embodied hope and joy, not hopelessness and despair. The ultimate purpose of SDI was to "free the world from the threat of nuclear war" by "rendering these nuclear weapons impotent and obsolete." In proposing

SDI, Reagan did not seek military or political superiority, but simply to make the world a safer and happier place in which to live.[10] These noble and ultimate purposes seem comforting and appropriate when yearning to create a less threatening world.

The strategic shift from scene to purpose in the speech represented an attempt at transcendence. The audience, fearful of the Soviets and concerned about the nuclear arms race, was symbolically lifted above the fray with SDI. The fear and worry associated with the material conditions of the scene were transcended by the chance of escaping from those dangerous conditions. An element of control over one's destiny entered the drama, for SDI purported to intercept and destroy missiles before they reached their targets. If MAD were to fail, Americans would not have to sit idly by and wait for the missiles to arrive. Rather, SDI would intervene and remove the threat. In such a symbolic construction, despair is replaced with hope, as the audience and the rhetor are united in their quest for the goal of eliminating the nuclear threat. SDI represented transcendence in another sense as well, in that Reagan envisioned it to be deployed in outer space, thus literally transcendent over material conditions.

When one particular pentadic term such as purpose is featured in discourse, all the others (scene, act, agent, and agency) must be made qualitatively and symbolically consistent with the dominant term, if the drama is to be coherent. If purpose is dominant, then acts, agents, and agencies described by the discourse must be congruent with the type of purpose strived for. In the case of Reagan's SDI program, the noble purpose of eliminating the threat of nuclear war serves to define the quality of acts, agents, and agencies necessary for the achievement of that purpose.

SDI was a fitting act, given the dramatic purpose and scene that Reagan developed; it was directed toward a "long-term research and development program to begin to achieve our ultimate goal of eliminating the threat posed by strategic nuclear missiles." It was a historic act, "an effort which holds the promise of changing the course of human history."[11] The creation of SDI was to be, therefore, a heroic effort, one that was noble and against the odds. But it was worth the risks, according to Reagan, given the dire situation in which the nation, and indeed the whole world, found itself.

Undertaking such a difficult and challenging act when confronted by a dangerous situation requires an agent that is competent, clever, and dedicated to the task. Reagan challenged the nation's brightest technical minds, the scientific community who gave us nuclear weapons in the first place, to "turn their great talents now to the cause of mankind and world peace."[12] These gifted Americans, with their world-renowned abilities and ingenuity, were appropriate agents for this difficult act, since it involved highly technical research and development efforts.

These researchers had at their disposal some very sophisticated, promising, and exciting means with which to achieve their goals. The appropriate agency for freeing the world from the threat of nuclear war, therefore, was to be found in "the very strengths in technology that spawned our great industrial base and that have given us the quality of life we enjoy today."[13] Reagan claimed that technology had reached a level of sophistication that made it the most appropriate means for effectively responding to the dangerous scene. He contended that the nation must "proceed boldly with these new technologies," and use them to eliminate the offensive missile threat.[14]

The drama embedded in Reagan's SDI discourse, then, is an adventurous and compelling one. Humanity is locked into a dangerous situation that is beyond its control. It is a situation of ultimate peril; if nuclear war were to occur, it would be an unimaginable catastrophe, with all living creatures as its victims. This situation is one of humanity's own making, however, in that human symbol use, intellect, and ingenuity made it possible to develop these machines of ultimate destruction. Humans, then, are not only the victims, but the heroes of the drama, for through the genius of technology, scientists can atone for their sins by developing a machine that will forever remove the threat of nuclear holocaust. These brave men and women are engaged in a quest to discover the secrets of strategic defense.

As expected, Reagan's "Star Wars" address launched a vigorous national debate over the feasibility and wisdom of SDI. As this debate progressed, subtle but important changes occurred in the administration's descriptions of the nature of the program and its rationale. The next portion of this chapter highlights these shifts in rationale in an attempt to explain the symbolic power of the strategic defense initiative and to describe different attempts by the Reagan administration to justify it.

SDI and America's Sense of Destiny

In Chapter 2, I explored various symbolic constructions of the history of the United States' foreign policy and argued that they reveal themes of American moral superiority, mission, and innocence. A sense of destiny, enacted through policies encouraging expansion and economic development into unknown frontiers, has been ingrained in these interpretations to some degree or another throughout American history. This strong sense of destiny and progress, coupled with idealism and innocence, was also evident in the Reagan Administration's SDI rhetoric.

The stated purpose of Reagan's SDI was to apply the talents and strengths of technicians, who supposedly created the nuclear threat, into a search for a technological solution to that threat. The drive for progress, implicit in American technological ingenuity, made expansion into the western frontier possible, and today it allows the nation to conquer new frontiers. Frontiers into outer space and frontiers of knowledge constitute the new American challenges, and Reagan's vision of SDI channeled some of the best American minds into meeting these challenges. According to the Reagan Administration, America's destiny and history of greatness would fuel public optimism as SDI researchers endeavored to meet these difficult challenges.

Lt. Gen. James A. Abrahamson, Director of the Strategic Defense Initiative Organization during the Reagan presidency, exhibited this technological optimism when he first testified before Congress in support of SDI in 1984. He argued, "I guess my experience as a technologist and as a manager with a long career in this effort is that we indeed can produce *miracles*" (emphasis mine.)[15] A Department of Defense document, provided to Congress, further reinforced the significance of technology in this effort when its authors asserted that "SDI will use America's greatest assets, our creativity and our ingenuity" in achieving its goals.[16] George A. Keyworth, Science Adviser to the President, put it even more bluntly, arguing that, while one can be either a pessimist or an optimist in these matters, he preferred optimism.[17] SDI advocates in this way celebrated technological optimism as a truly American trait. Reagan argued that trimming the SDI budget over doubts about its feasibility "would run counter to the American spirit that pushed back frontiers in all realms of endeavor."[18] Kenneth Adelman, Director of the Arms Control and Disarmament Agency, claimed: "This approach is quintessentially American—holding out an objective which is right and beneficial and then working diligently to make it happen. SDI has become an American challenge."[19]

By mustering the forces of optimism and Americanism, SDI advocates were able to label opponents pessimists, and, by implication, unpatriotic. Former Secretary of Defense, Casper Weinberger, called upon a sense of history to support his plea for technological optimism, when he argued:

> The nay-sayers have already proclaimed that we will never have such technology, or that we should never try to acquire it. Their arguments are hardly new.... In 1945 President Truman's Chief of Staff, Admiral William Leahy, said of the atomic bomb: "That's the biggest fool thing we've ever done. The bomb will never go off, and I speak as an expert in explosives."[20]

In other words, either one can have faith in America's greatest strengths and support SDI research, or one can be a "nay-sayer." Reagan joined in on the attack, arguing that the "nay-sayers" and "the blame-America-first crowd," with "their steady drumbeat of doubt and distaste" questioned the feasibility of SDI.[21] According to John Gardner, Director of the Systems Division of the Strategic Defense Initiative Organization, some scientific nay-sayers, who changed their minds and decided to support SDI, were "intellectually honest enough to be capable of being persuaded by technical facts and calculations."[22]

Advocates' pleas for technological optimism were grounded in both historical and scientific claims. Reagan argued that American history is replete with dramatic accounts of technological breakthroughs in industry, agriculture, and medicine. America's greatest technological heroes, including Thomas Edison, the Wright brothers, and Alexander Graham Bell, he argued, were not daunted by the technological pessimists of their day.[23] By calling upon these examples of American genius, Reagan called forth a compelling sense of history, and used it to support his calls for faith in SDI research.

In 1986, Reagan began to speak of breakthroughs appearing specifically in SDI research. He contended that technological advances in sensors and homing devices resulted in "even faster progress than expected."[24] These advances showed promise in a difficult area of ballistic missile defense, detecting and tracking a missile during its early boost phase. If missiles could be destroyed during this boost phase, difficult technical problems associated with interception and destruction at later phases of missile flight would be avoided. These breakthroughs allowed Reagan to proclaim that, when given a choice between trusting the Soviets and trusting American technology, "I'll put my money on American technology anytime."[25] In this way, Reagan reenacted the historical and quintessentially American drama of technological breakthroughs in the face of seemingly insurmountable odds before the nation's very eyes. Proponents of SDI were united as one with this great history of American destiny and progress.

From this perspective, the transcendent purpose of SDI, as outlined by Reagan in the "Star Wars" speech, is achieved through the agency of applied science. The pentadic term "agency" corresponds with the philosophy of pragmatism. Discourse emphasizing agency, then, focuses upon the instruments used to achieve particular ends.[26] The rise of science in the modern world represents a cultural privileging of agency, in that technology is called upon to solve all social ills. In Reagan's SDI rhetoric, though, agency and purpose seem to merge: technology produces "miracles" as a god would; it is its own justification, in that it is intrinsically "American" and good. It is simultaneously means and ends.

Technology, of course, provided humanity with the means of destroying all life, in the form of nuclear weapons. Although dependent upon technology, the SDI program was presented as a benign application of the logic of science. The Reagan Administration described it as merely a research program, and one that would serve the noble purposes of finding ways to render nuclear weapons impotent and obsolete, or, at a minimum, make nuclear war less likely. SDI was to be carried out in accordance with all treaty obligations. Most importantly, it sought to develop only a defen-

sive weapon. Reagan emphasized that the SDI program sought a nonnuclear, purely defensive system. It would be a nonnuclear "security shield"
that wouldn't kill people, but rather, destroy weapons.[27] In fact, he
claimed, "Weapon isn't the term to use for what we're researching."[28] It
was a "high-tech shield" and "an insurance policy for your future."[29] By
defining the program as nonnuclear and purely defensive, Reagan shielded
himself against critics who claimed that the SDI program would trigger
the militarization of outer space.

The administration realized, however, that a system like SDI, in the
hands of an aggressive nation, would be dangerous. If coupled with strong
and accurate offensive forces, ballistic missile defenses could provide the
missing element in an aggressive nuclear first strike posture.[30] A nation
with ulterior motives could launch a surprise attack, and protect itself
from retaliation with its defensive systems. Reagan emphasized, however,
that his administration did not seek military superiority, or have aggressive motives, in pursuing SDI. He claimed that the United States would
not use it to support a first strike posture because to do so would be
inconsistent with the nation's self-image and traditions.[31] Whether these
arguments were sufficient enough to persuade the Soviets of Reagan's
peaceful intentions is another matter. But by linking SDI to a perceived
tradition of American nonaggression and innocence, Reagan attempted to
strengthen the symbolic appeal of the program for domestic audiences.

SDI's grounding in America's historical destiny, optimism, and innocence provided distinct rhetorical advantages for proponents of the program. Those who doubted the technical feasibility of SDI were presented
with historical evidence of past nay-sayers who were proven wrong. They
were called pessimists and doubters, and were contrasted with those who
had hope for the future. An optimistic, hopeful vision of the future would
seem to be more appealing than a pessimistic one, given its linkages with
Reagan's interpretation of the nation's past experiences.

When discussing the first strike implications of SDI, opponents of the
program were faced with another difficult task. To argue against SDI on
the basis that it provided the United States with a first strike capability,
one had to be willing to assume that U. S. leaders could be capable of such
an action. That American decision makers might initiate, deliberately and

with careful planning, an all-out nuclear war is probably unthinkable to most American audiences. Such an action would violate the nation's perceived standards of morality and would be tantamount to genocide. It seems that Americans are more likely to accept far-fetched technological claims about SDI's feasibility than far-fetched moral claims about a United States nuclear first strike. As long as SDI remains closely linked with typically American notions of progress, morality, and innocence, it will be difficult for opponents to formulate equally effective and compelling arguments to rebut it.

SDI and the Nuclear Freeze Campaign

Reagan's call for strategic defense was also symbolically powerful in that it captured much of the persuasive appeal of nuclear disarmament and the nuclear freeze proposal. Many of the rhetorical themes that guided and motivated nuclear freeze supporters are found in pro-SDI rhetoric, and some of the rhetorical weaknesses of the nuclear freeze proposal were addressed by Reagan's notion of strategic defense. Proclaimed by the administration to be a safer way to achieve the benefits of nuclear disarmament, SDI offered even more hope for a future free of the nuclear threat than did the nuclear freeze proposal.

Even though the technology of strategic defense and its implications for nuclear doctrine and strategy are quite complex, the notion of intercepting and destroying ballistic missiles appeals to common sense. As I argued in chapter 3, the nuclear freeze campaign, which called for the superpowers to end the arms race by adopting a moratorium on the testing, production, and deployment of new weapons systems, appealed to the common sense of the American public. Similarly, SDI, at least in its most optimistic form (a complete, leakproof population defense), appealed to common sense. In his "Star Wars" address, for example, Reagan claimed that it would be better to save lives than to avenge them, that defense is better and safer than offense, and that making nuclear weapons impotent and obsolete is preferable to freezing the U. S. into a position of strategic inferiority.[32] In a June, 1986 speech, Reagan went even further and argued that SDI would be "a shield that could protect us from nuclear missiles just as a roof protects a family from rain."[33] Common sense dictates that parents would want to shield their children from the storm; in Reagan's view, this same common sense supported SDI.

The public's fear of nuclear war, which obviously was important in the discourse of the nuclear freeze campaign, was also important in SDI rhetoric. In their descriptions of scene, Reagan and his advisers bemoaned what they saw as the immorality and danger inherent in MAD. In a press conference, for example, Reagan claimed "it is inconceivable...that the great nations of the world will sit here, like people facing themselves across a table, each with a cocked gun, and no one knowing whether someone might tighten their finger on the trigger."[34] The Hoffman Panel, created by Reagan to assess the strategic and political implications of SDI, contended that the reliance solely on offensive retaliation to keep the peace was "increasingly hollow and morally unacceptable."[35] SDI research, therefore, became a moral imperative, even if it offered only a glimmer of hope. As Abrahamson argued, "The mere promise of such options may remove the pall of fear and anxiety that overshadows our young and provide them with the confidence that their future need not be dominated by the overriding fear of nuclear destruction."[36] SDI would provide more comfort to a fearful public than a nuclear freeze, in that it would offer a future free of MAD, which keeps the world indefinitely teetering on the brink of annihilation. A nuclear freeze, on the other hand, would deliberately maintain that threat of annihilation as a potentially permanent condition.

SDI appeared to make the world safer than a nuclear freeze by addressing another strong public concern: fear and distrust of the Soviet Union. Ever since the Cold War, Americans were told that the Soviets were fanatically ideological, bent on world domination and a threat to traditional American values. As recently as 1983, in fact, Reagan referred to the Soviet Union as "the focus of evil in the modern world" and an "evil empire."[37] As an insurance policy against Soviet treaty violations, SDI relieved both the fear of nuclear war and the Soviet threat simultaneously. According to SDI advocates, the Soviets conducted extensive research into the same technologies envisioned by SDI and actually deployed some of them.[38] These advocates argued that continuation and expansion of the American SDI research program was vital as a hedge against a Soviet breakout of the 1972 Antiballistic Missile Treaty, which severely limited testing and deployment of systems like SDI.

If the Soviet Union, "which has the most and greatest nuclear weapons arsenal in the world, also had with it a defense against nuclear weapons," Reagan claimed, the dangerous situation of the present would look even more ominous.[39] From this perspective, the purpose of SDI was consistent with the purpose of every other major weapons system: to protect American security, values, and way of life. As Reagan argued, "our SDI research program is crucial to maintain the military balance and protect the liberty and freedom of the West."[40] Someday, even "a madman like Qadaffi" or a terrorist group might be armed with nuclear weapons.[41] In a world as dangerous as this one, with the enemies of freedom growing stronger every day, SDI proponents argued that the United States could not afford to be without some sort of ballistic missile defense system.

Nuclear freeze supporters argued that the arsenals of the superpowers were enormous and that such "overkill" was not only unnecessary, but dangerous. They also claimed that traditional arms control techniques failed to address the escalating nuclear arms race. As I explained in chapter 3, they argued that a nuclear arms freeze would create a stable political and symbolic environment in which productive disarmament negotiations would have a real chance for success. They concluded, therefore, that a drastic break from traditional arms control dogma was necessary if there was to be hope for the future. Reagan claimed, however, that the SDI program would provide the leverage needed to bring the Soviets to the negotiating table. Initially, this claim appeared as if SDI ultimately would be a kind of bargaining chip, traded away at some later date in exchange for arms control concessions. In 1985, however, Reagan made it clear that this was not the case.[42] He argued that SDI would not be negotiated away as part of a deal for offensive weapons. On the contrary, if at some later time it became a feasible and effective system, Reagan claimed, he would be willing to give SDI technology to the rest of the world, and hope that it would be a sufficient incentive to eliminate offensive nuclear missiles.[43]

Reagan also argued that he would not unilaterally deploy this system if proven feasible, but would sit down with allies and adversaries alike and consult with them on developing a transition to a purely defensive strategic environment. Speaking with European reporters, Reagan stated, "We would ultimately make a decision on whether to deploy strategic defense systems only after consultations with our allies and negotiations with the Soviet Union, as envisioned by the ABM Treaty."[44] If such negotiations ever took place, Reagan claimed, he would "see if we cannot come to an agreement on which there will be deployment [of SDI] only if there is elimination of the nuclear weapons."[45]

In 1986, any remaining uncertainty over SDI's status as a bargaining chip apparently was settled when, at the superpower summit meeting in Reykjavik, Iceland, Reagan refused to negotiate away SDI in exchange for drastic cuts in offensive nuclear arsenals. In an address to the nation, Reagan defended his decision, claiming, "SDI is America's insurance policy that the Soviet Union would keep the commitments made at Reykjavik."[46]

Reagan's stance concerning the bargaining chip issue is admittedly ambiguous and complex, but it is also rhetorically interesting. Reagan proposed a drastic change in the way arms control traditionally operates by initiating an intensive and highly publicized effort to develop ballistic missile defense. He argued that such drastic action was necessary in order to persuade the Soviets to get serious about arms control. He offered hope for drastic offensive weapon reductions *in the long-term*, but at the same time, he refused to allow his project to be traded away for *short-term* offensive reductions. In this way, Reagan allowed SDI to function symbolically as a bargaining chip, while refusing to even consider giving it away at the negotiating table. He held out hope for nuclear disarmament in the future without actually dismantling a single intercontinental ballistic missile. He captured the long-term appeal of a nuclear freeze without backing away from his commitment to SDI.

In Reagan's view, therefore, SDI was a more realistic and complete solution to the problems addressed by the nuclear freeze proposal. It relieved the public's fear of nuclear war by ensuring that the missiles would never reach their targets. It did not require trust in the Soviet Union to comply with any agreements.

Upon closer examination, however, Reagan's apparently naive and simplistic view of SDI was not necessarily shared by his advisers, who were much more aware of the technical issues involved in the research. Ambiguity surrounding the strategic objectives of SDI (whether it was intended to protect cities or missile silos) is a key element of inconsistency that emerges in an analysis of the Administration's discourse. This inconsistency is perhaps the most important issue in this discussion, in that Reagan's noble and benign version of SDI is called into question when compared with the less noble, and more dangerous, version advocated by his technical advisers.

In Reagan's original address, it seemed that his purpose in proposing SDI was to free the world from offensive nuclear forces by rendering them impotent and obsolete with a defensive system that would operate like a shield. This optimistic goal of a comprehensive population defense that would protect American cities was maintained by former Secretary of Defense, Caspar Weinberger, who claimed that: "the defensive systems the President is talking about are not designed to be partial," and that the administration would try to develop a system "that is so reliable that it will, in effect, render impotent all of these nuclear missiles."[47]

Other advocates, however, envisioned a more limited SDI program. Both Abrahamson and the Department of Defense described SDI technologies as methods for strengthening deterrence by creating uncertainties in the mind of an attacker.[48] According to these sources, if SDI technologies were proven feasible, even at significantly less than one hundred percent effectiveness, an adversary determined to carry out a nuclear first strike against the United States would not be certain that the attack would "succeed," given that it would not be able to predict how many missiles would penetrate the defenses and reach their targets. According to this logic, the hypothetical adversary would be deterred from initiating an attack in the first place.

It is unclear which of these views represented the guiding objective of the SDI program. Statements by Reagan concerning the goals of the research illustrate this uncertainty. At a February, 1985 press conference, Reagan was asked whether he was pursuing a leakproof population defense. He responded:

> Oh, I've never asked for one hundred percent. That would be a
> fine goal, but you can have a most effective defensive weapon
> even if it isn't one hundred percent, because what you would

have is the knowledge that—or that the other fellow would have the knowledge that if they launched a first strike, that it might be such that not enough of their missiles could get through and in return we could launch the retaliatory strike.[49]

In this statement, Reagan seemed to accept the rationale proposed by Abrahamson and the Department of Defense, that SDI would strengthen deterrence by protecting America's ability to retaliate. In his very next sentence, however, Reagan said, "Now, that isn't really the goal of the Strategic Defense Initiative," which he claimed was the ultimate elimination of all nuclear weapons.[50]

Two weeks later, when asked by a reporter whether he wanted point defense protecting missile silos or a more complete defense protecting cities, Reagan said:

I want a defense that simply says that if somebody starts pushing the button on those weapons, we've got a good chance of keeping all or at least the bulk of them from getting to the target. Because, even if it's around missile sites, that's the type of weapon anymore in which there's no way to restrain that from killing any number of people....[51]

Here, Reagan seemed to concede that SDI would probably only defend missile sites, but he implied that even if that were the case, many civilian lives would be saved. What he failed to mention, however, is that those very missiles that escaped destruction would then be launched against Soviet targets in retaliation. This guaranteed retaliatory capability, according to Reagan's technical advisers, would supposedly deter the Soviets from ever launching an attack in the first place. In this way, Reagan's moral purpose became immersed in the technostrategic logic of nuclear deterrence. In April, 1985, however, Reagan reversed his position again, claiming that SDI was a way to break out of mutually assured destruction, and that "this is not and should never be misconstrued as just another method of protecting missile silos."[52]

Not only were the objectives of the program unclear, but the goals of enhancing deterrence by complicating Soviet first strike plans and protecting missile silos were inconsistent with what seemed to be Reagan's original goal, protecting Americans directly with defensive systems. Reagan's ideal version of SDI was one where the complicated logic of MAD would be transcended by eliminating the need for offensive nuclear forces. Abrahamson's version was a supplement to the logic of MAD, ensuring that attacks were deterred by guaranteeing that sufficient U. S. offensive forces would survive to retaliate.

This ambiguity in objectives became even more apparent when the conclusions of the Hoffman Panel revealed that the most likely long-term result of SDI would be a U. S. nuclear force structure characterized by a mix of offensive missiles and defensive systems.[53] Reagan continued to maintain that his goal was the complete elimination of offensive ballistic missiles, while his advisers claimed that the United States would have to maintain a strong offensive missile force, even if SDI were deployed and fully operational.[54]

There are two possible explanations for these ambiguities. Either Reagan was misleading American audiences when he advocated a complete population defense, or he had little or no understanding of the intricacies of nuclear strategy and doctrine. His optimistic dream of a shield that would protect Americans from missiles, like a roof protects a family from rain, is simply not technically feasible. But he continued to maintain that dream when publicly discussing the SDI program. It is unknown whether American audiences accepted Reagan's dream, or the more limited version actually being pursued by SDI researchers, as the "true" SDI program. But Reagan's vision, with its optimism, hopefulness, and simplicity, would seem to be appealing to citizens fearful of the risk of nuclear war, and confused by the logic of MAD.

SDI, Symbol Use, and Innocence

At several points in this study, I have hinted at some of the deeper symbolic implications of SDI. It is appropriate at this point to draw these ideas together, and develop a clearer explanation of why Reagan's version of SDI may be appealing to humans as symbol-using creatures, who define themselves through language.

In chapter 1, I argued that a symbolic, rhetorical approach to the study of nuclear war is appropriate, since most of what is known about the subject is symbolically constructed. A full-scale nuclear exchange has not occurred; therefore, symbolic expression constitutes virtually the entire stock of human experience with nuclear war. Since nuclear war is symbolically constructed, humans have great freedom to define what it is and to adjust interpretations of it to fit material circumstances. In this way, symbol use implies great freedom, for language enables humans to search creatively for solutions to problems. To illustrate the freedom engendered by symbol use, Burke provided an anecdote about a bird trapped in a classroom, flying in circles close to the ceiling, while windows were open only a few inches below. If only the bird were able to speak, and humans could speak its language, Burke claimed, a simple statement could solve its problem: "Fly down just a foot or so, and out one of those windows."[55] Through the genius of symbol use, therefore, humans have freedoms denied other creatures. These very freedoms can aid people in their search for solutions to the nuclear arms race.

Paradoxically, however, symbol use itself creates constraints on human freedom. The ability to use symbols makes humans the "inventor[s] of the negative," and, thus, creates the resulting codes of moral conduct and hierarchies that constrain human action. Symbol use, according to Burke, represents at its core a desire for control and perfection, of which humans inevitably fall short. This unfulfilled desire for perfection and order leads to guilt, in Burke's terminology, which must be purged through more symbol use. In other words, the freedom inherent in symbolicity can never be completely and fully realized; hierarchy, guilt, and disorder are inevitable by-products of symbol use.

This paradox represents the irony implicit in one clause of Burke's *Definition of Man*, that humans are separated from their natural condition by instruments of their own making.[56] Human beings are literally set apart from nature, due to the wonders of modern technology (which result from the use of symbols). But in another sense, the instruments of our own making—symbols—serve to alienate us, in that they constrain our actions. Humans want to escape from the implications of symbol use (guilt, hierarchy, the negative, etc.), but can only attempt to do so through symbol use itself. In theological terms, symbol use is analogous to the fall from Eden; the innocence of Adam and Eve was lost when knowledge of good and evil was bestowed by the serpent. Once that innocence was lost, however, it could only be restored through redemption. In secular terms, humans strive for redemption through symbols, forever yearning for the innocence available only to non-symbol-using creatures.[57]

Reagan's utopian vision of SDI appealed to symbol-using creatures in part because it seemingly offered a way out of this dilemma. In Reagan's SDI drama, machines fight other machines in a battle to save the world from nuclear peril. Technology is the hero in this drama, as its human creators appear to sieze the initiative, take control, and develop a machine that frees humanity from it's terrible mistake: the invention of nuclear weapons. Goaded by hierarchy, and rotten with perfection, these symbol-using creatures were bound to push their symbolicity to the end of the line and develop machines capable of destroying symbol use itself. But by turning to a technological solution to the arms race (SDI), humans are finally absolved of that guilt by acquiring the ability to destroy the destroyer.

As a purely technological solution, moreover, SDI provides a way out of the negative implications of symbol use, in that it exists in the realm of motion, not action. Burke argues that there is a distinction between "action" and "sheer motion." He contends that: "'Action' is a term for the kind of behavior possible to a typically symbol-using animal (such as man [sic]) in contrast with the extrasymbolic or nonsymbolic operations of nature."[58] Action involves human choice and decision, motion does not. Machines like SDI exist in the realm of motion; once they are switched on by human agents, they operate independently of human choice and decision. In this sense, then, SDI represents a complete surrender to the realm of motion. With SDI, the responsibilities inherent in human action are avoided, as are the guilt and hierarchy inherent in symbol use.

In this way, SDI offers a return not only to pre-nuclear but also presymbolic innocence. By surrendering the freedom to use symbols creatively to negotiate an end to the arms race, SDI supporters offer to free Americans from the pain and difficulty associated with symbolic action. But this innocence has its dark side, in that it seems almost Orwellian, for in this case, Americans actively choose to give up the freedom of symbolicity. By choosing the least painful and least demanding alternative, SDI advocates avoid the paradox of symbolicity, but simultaneously give up the human elements of decision and action.

This apparent transcendence of the dilemmas of symbol use, however, is merely an illusion. SDI is, as are all other proposed solutions to the arms race, inherently symbolic. Not only is SDI itself the product of symbol use (technology), but all we know of it is symbolic. Words about SDI lead to the same dramatistic implications as do words about disarmament; hierarchy, guilt, and the desire for perfection. The irony of SDI's appeal, therefore, is that it appears to transcend these dilemmas, while remaining firmly embedded in them.

Public Debate and Technical Uncertainty

An examination of the Reagan Administration's SDI rhetoric illustrates how difficult it can be for public debate to influence nuclear weapons policy-making. In an ideal, and perhaps naive sense, citizens and elected officials in a democratic nation should engage in open and robust public debate when faced with a proposal like SDI. Defensive systems have important implications for strategic stability, in that if one nation deploys defenses and others do not, the nation with defenses can carry out an attack without fear of retaliation. In this way, the entire foundation of strategic stability would be undermined. In addition, the nation without defenses would be rightfully concerned about the forthcoming deployment, and may be tempted to attack the system even before completion. Even if both adversaries possessed defensive systems, some argue that strategic stability would be undermined, since American war planners would not be able to predict how many retaliatory warheads would be able to penetrate enemy defenses, even if they survived an initial enemy attack.[59]

Given these serious concerns, opponents of the program must be provided an opportunity to question and challenge the administration's view, in order to understand fully the nature, costs, and objectives of the program. Opportunities for robust debate are provided, of course, in forums such as public speeches, Congressional hearings, and the popular press. But on close examination, these opportunities for debate over SDI were not fruitful during the Reagan presidency, because it was described as only a research program and, whenever it was challenged, its advocates asserted that the technologies involved were only just emerging.

Ever since SDI was announced in 1983, administration sources emphasized vehemently that it was a research program, designed to determine whether development and deployment of ballistic missile defenses might be feasible sometime in the future.[60] They maintained that any future decision on deployment would be a national decision made by a future president and Congress. As time goes on, however, it appears that such a decision in favor of some type of deployment may be inevitable. As billions of dollars are committed to SDI research, and as hundreds of contracts with defense manufacturers are negotiated, the bureaucratic, institutional, and financial momentum in favor of SDI grows. Once such a large investment is made in a weapons system, it is difficult to stop its deployment. This progression towards deployment of SDI was evident not only in financial and contractual terms, but also in the rhetoric of the Reagan administration.

A close reading of the Reagan administration's SDI discourse reveals hints of gradual movement away from pure laboratory research and toward actual development and deployment of an SDI system. This rhetorical progression is vaguely evident in public revelations of amazing technological breakthroughs, and in Reagan's unwillingness to negotiate the program away at Reykjavik in exchange for drastic offensive reductions. In 1987 and early 1988, these hints became much more explicit. The controversy concerning the so-called "broad interpretation" of the ABM Treaty, and explicit statements by Reagan and his advisers about deployment, illustrated this move.

In late 1985, the White House legal adviser, Abraham Sofaer, discovered that aspects of the negotiating history of the 1972 ABM Treaty could be interpreted as allowing broader discretion in testing defensive components than had been thought earlier.[61] In 1987, it appeared that the administration was moving officially to adopt this broader interpretation of the treaty limitations. Many in Congress took this as a sign that SDI research had progressed to a stage where it was necessary either to redefine the treaty or violate it, in order to continue SDI research. Although the White House claimed that this new interpretation of the treaty did not affect the current SDI research program in any way, administration sources acknowledged that at some time in the future it may be necessary to adopt it.[62] This created significant controversy in Congress, and arms control advocates attempted to pass legislation that would bind the administration to the treaty's more narrow interpretation.

Other evidence of an intent to deploy an SDI system can be found in explicit statements by Reagan and his staff. In mid-1988, both Reagan and former Secretary of State, George Schultz, publicly argued that if it were proven feasible, SDI would be deployed.[63] In late 1987, research in the SDI Organization's laboratories had progressed to the point where Abrahamson was able to send detailed descriptions of a "strawman" system called Phase 1 to the Department of Defense for analysis and approval.[64] Phase 1 would be a partial defense system, with limited capabilities, but Abrahamson stressed that it could "deny the Soviets a cheap strike," and, therefore, would help to deter a surprise attack.[65]

But if the program was, and officially still is, merely a research effort, how did this apparent momentum toward actual development and deployment come about? One answer can be found by exploring further the "rhetoric of research" found in pro-SDI discourse. By emphasizing that the program was merely scientific laboratory research, SDI advocates developed a rhetorical posture that was insulated against strong challenge, and provided self-perpetuating momentum for the program.

The speculative nature of the technologies involved in SDI research made it difficult for opponents to develop a strong case against it. Since many important technical and strategic questions concerning missile defense could not be answered without further research, the program was insulated from criticism. Uncertainty, rather than a reason *not* to act, became a *call to* act. Proponents could argue simultaneously that SDI was probably technically feasible, and that research should proceed to make sure that it was. Opponents, however, could not logically contend that it wasn't possible, and that research shouldn't proceed, since further study could potentially prove them wrong. Excerpts from Congressional committee hearings on SDI provide dramatic illustrations of this problem.

In hearings before the Senate Committee on Foreign Relations on April 25, 1984, Lt. Gen. Abrahamson, Dr. Robert S. Cooper, Director of the Defense Advanced Research Projects Agency, and Richard N. Perle, Assistant Secretary of Defense for International Security Policy testified in support of SDI. When asked by Senator Paul Tsongas of Massachussetts whether the systems envisioned for SDI would allow enough time for a human decision maker to initiate the operation of the defensive system, Cooper responded:

> No one knows what a future system design might be like. It could be possible that if tensions had risen and we were at DEFCON 4 or 5, that the President would be available and could make decisions on a few-minutes time scale. But no one knows the answer to your question. No one knows exactly what the system design would be or what technology it would employ to put the command and control authorities into a position where they could start and stop the system.[66]

Unsatisfied with this answer, Senator Joseph Biden of Delaware pursued the question by creating a hypothetical scenario in which the United States was under a surprise nuclear attack. He asked Cooper whether human decision making would be possible, given the likelihood that the president would not have immediate access to command and control facilities in the two or three minutes necessary to activate the system. Cooper responded by saying, "You are creating artificial phantoms that you want to shoot down. What we are saying is that your artificial phantom is of no consequence. No one knows what that future will be like."[67] Biden then asked Cooper to assume for the moment that the detection of a surprise attack was in error, a computer malfunction. Cooper responded, "We are not ready to assume that, because we don't know [whether or not] in that time period we couldn't create technologies that would not make such a mistake possible." To this, Biden responded, "You have convinced me that I don't want the program in the hands of a man like you." The questioning ended.[68]

In this situation, members of Congress, who were knowledgeable about national security issues and United States nuclear policies, attempted to ask important and challenging questions about SDI. They wanted to know how a potential SDI system would operate, and whether it would allow enough time for human decision makers to actively choose to initiate operation of the system. Their efforts were frustrated, however, by Cooper's insistence that the research had not progressed to a stage where he could answer such questions. Given that no one knew what potential systems eventually would be deployed, the Senators' questions were dismissed as irrelevant.

Another example of this problem occurred when Tsongas asked whether the Soviet Union could potentially, and dangerously, misperceive an SDI system to be an antisatellite weapon. Cooper responded by arguing:

> All of these issues which you are bringing up, which I think are spurious issues at this stage of the game, are issues that will be addressed by the research program, and all of those issues will have to be suitably accounted for and taken care of in our research program, or no system will be possible.[69]

In other words, Cooper contended that those who were intimately involved in the research program, who had the most at stake if it failed, were to be the ones responsible for carrying out robust public debate over the potential policy implications of deployment of an SDI system. The implication was that elected officials, such as Tsongas and Biden, were not to challenge the system until more public funds had been committed to undertake more research.

But given that the technology was still emerging and that the program was designed to answer research questions, Congressional decision makers who had to decide whether to provide billions of dollars in funding for SDI did so under conditions of great uncertainty. When asked the potential cost of developing and deploying an SDI system, an administration researcher, Fred S. Hoffman responded, "I do not believe that the state of the understanding of the SDI has proceeded far enough so that we can conduct precise cost and effectiveness calculations at this time.[70] Even at the stage where a Phase 1 system had been postulated, cost and effectiveness estimates were described by Abrahamson as highly speculative and uncertain.[71]

In this situation, where Congressional support is granted under conditions of speculation and uncertainty, accountability for decisions concerning development and deployment of an SDI system is non-existent. In this case, researchers are their own watchdogs, while Congress and the public are denied the right to monitor the disbursement of public funds. A good example of this lack of accountability is the controversy over the x-ray laser system. The technological optimism surrounding this system, when coupled with extreme secrecy due to the highly classified nature of the research, created an embarrassing situation for Lawrence Livermore National Laboratories, based at the University of California, Berkeley.

Dr. Roy Woodruff, Director of the x-ray laser program at Livermore, resigned his post in October, 1985, in protest over the conduct of the research effort. Woodruff alleged that Dr. Edward Teller, father of the hydrogen bomb, and his protege, Dr. Lowell Wood, had collaborated in efforts to conduct secret high-level briefings at the White House concerning the x-ray laser program. Woodruff believed that these briefings were overly optimistic and technically inaccurate, in that they provided exaggerated reports concerning the advancement of the research.[72] Even though a federal investigation was launched to explore these allegations, administration speakers publicly urged nuclear weapons scientists to keep their differences quiet.[73] Such recommendations served to further insulate SDI and other weapons programs from public debate and discussion.

In the final analysis, insulation from public scrutiny and lack of accountability suggests that the SDI program gained symbolic and institutional momentum during the Reagan Administration that may be difficult to arrest. The program in essence became self-perpetuating as uncertainty called for more research, and the results of that research created more uncertainty, calling for still more research. Such self-perpetuating momentum was evident in a Department of Defense statement reporting that important SDI studies "recognized that there are uncertainties that will not be resolved until more is known.... These uncertainties notwithstanding, the studies concluded that it was essential that options for the deployment of advanced ballistic missile defenses be established."[74] A pamphlet released by the White House was even more explicit, claiming: "Arguments made by Western scientists over the feasibility of defending against ballistic missiles can only be resolved with further research."[75]

Conclusion

Since the end of Ronald Reagan's presidency, profound and significant changes have occurred in the international arena. Given the end of the Cold War, the war in the Persian Gulf, the failed Soviet coup attempt, and the increasing concern over ballistic missile and nuclear weapons proliferation, how is the Bush Administration attempting to justify the continuation of SDI research? What happens to a program which was grounded in fears of the Soviet Union, when such fears have abated? In the next chapter, I explore these questions, and identify ways in which the Bush Administration's discourse justifying SDI builds upon Reagan's vision, and, in fact, calls upon similarly appealing rhetorical forms.

5.
The "New World Order" and SDI

THE STRATEGIC DEFENSE INITIATIVE was Ronald Reagan's pet project. His vision of protecting Americans from nuclear armed ballistic missiles merged nicely with his distrust of the Soviet "evil empire," his optimistic outlook on life, his faith in American technological ingenuity, and his nostalgic view of the United States and its history. But what about his successor, George Bush? Given the end of the Cold War, the changing international scene marked by increasing multipolarity, fears about the proliferation of weapons of mass destruction with sophisticated ballistic missile delivery systems, and the 1991 war in the Persian Gulf, what role does the Strategic Defense Initiative play in the Bush presidency? How is the program represented in the era of a "new world order?" In this chapter, I explore the emerging symbolic constructions of SDI in the Bush administration, given these changing world conditions.

A dramatistic analysis of the discourse of Bush administration officials reveals that the rhetorical form of Reagan's utopian vision of strategic defense, namely a dark and dangerous international scene that could be transcended through investment in high technology solutions to the nuclear arms race, was similar to the rhetorical form evident in the Bush administration's foreign policy discourse. I shall argue that Bush's representations of Saddam Hussein of Iraq, as an evil, aggressive dictator who savagely brutalized a peaceful neighbor, were similar to Reagan's representations of the Soviet Union in the early 1980s. Bush's discourse during the Gulf War revealed his faith in America's destiny and mission to save the world from the scourge of war and aggression, just as Reagan's SDI discourse was grounded in a similar faith. Bush's call for a "new world order" represented an attempt at transcendence over a dark and dangerous scene, as he developed a rhetorical progression through dimensions of time and space, that was juxtaposed against the regressive and uncivilized policies of Iraq, and metaphorically, other "Third World" nations. The administration's discourse during the Persian Gulf War, with its images of new and dangerous enemies, provided a compelling symbolic context for Bush's reconceptualization of SDI, Global Protection Against Limited Strikes (GPALS). Although described through the same rhetorical forms used by Reagan, Bush's symbolic constructions of the enemy were perhaps even more discursively violent in that they reproduced and reified the ideology of colonialism, shifted the language of the East-West confrontation into the rhetorical and material conflicts between North and South, and, thereby, strengthened United States hegemony in a changing world.

SDI and the End of the Cold War

During the 1988 presidential campaign, George Bush did not seem as enamored of SDI as his predecessor. Fred Barnes argued that Bush was always "lukewarm" on SDI, in that he did not believe that Reagan's concept of a "peace shield" to protect Americans from ballistic missiles was technically feasible.[1] The focus of the Bush administration's early efforts towards the Strategic Defense Initiative were directed at research, in order to determine whether deployment of a system would even be feasible.[2] Although Bush's initial budget request for fiscal year 1990 was the same as Reagan's, $5.6 billion, his administration's support for continued budgetary emphasis on SDI seemed to waver in subsequent public statements and funding requests.[3] While fighting for confirmation of his nomination as Secretary of Defense before the Senate Armed Services Committee, John Tower expressed his doubts concerning Reagan's broad conception of SDI. He contended that the Bush administration did not consider it possible to "devise an umbrella that can protect the entire American population from nuclear incineration."[4] Later statements indicated that Bush and his advisers were taking a more modest view of SDI, perhaps embracing only a land-based system to defend missile installations.[5] The administration's final 1990 budget request for SDI—$4.8 billion, rather than the

$5.6 billion originally proposed—indicated that Bush was perhaps not as enthusiastic about strategic defense as was Reagan.[6]

Once firmly in office, however, Administration officials contended that their intentions towards SDI were the same as Reagan's; continued research and eventual deployment of a system to protect against ballistic missile attack. Richard Burt, chief negotiator for the Strategic Arms Reduction Talks (START), argued:

> Similarly, President Bush has decided that our goals remain unchanged. The SDI program will continue to research, develop, and test concepts for effective defenses in full compliance with the Antiballistic Missile (ABM) Treaty. In defense and space, we will preserve our options to deploy advanced defenses when they are ready.[7]

Similarly, Henry F. Cooper, soon to become the Director of the SDI Organization, argued that Bush directed him to "preserve U. S. options to develop and deploy advanced defenses when they are ready" in his negotiating efforts with the Soviets in the Defense and Space Talks.[8] Even Bush himself seemed to embrace Reagan's vision of strategic defense when, in July, 1989, he claimed that "we are committed to deploy when ready a more comprehensive defensive system, known as SDI," and that the premise of the program was clear, that defensive weapons endangered no person, and no country.[9]

The rhetorical challenges faced by the officials advocating SDI, however, were twofold. First, immense changes were beginning to take place inside the Soviet Union and in Eastern Europe. Given that Reagan's SDI discourse was grounded in concerns about the Soviet military threat, calls to continue the program under the same premises seemed like a throwback to a distant era. Second, the relaxation of tensions between the United States and the Soviet Union resulted in public and Congressional hopes for a "peace dividend," a chance to reduce defense spending and concentrate on funding programs to relieve domestic ills such as poverty, illiteracy, homelessness, and a crumbling educational system. These concerns were echoed in the halls of Congress, and resulted in budgetary difficulties for Bush's plans for the Strategic Defense Initiative.

As I argued in previous chapters, Reagan's claim in 1982 that the Soviet Union was an evil empire bent on world domination was persuasive to many American citizens, and resulted in ambivalent support at best for the nuclear freeze proposal. Images of Soviet aggression in Afghanistan, coupled with Reagan's crusading rhetoric of the Cold War, intensified during the early 1980s. But Mikhail Gorbachev's rise to power in the Soviet Union seemed to challenge these characterizations. He embarked on a massive program to reform the Soviet system through sweeping political, military, and economic changes. The world witnessed the collapse of the Warsaw Pact, the unification of Germany, and the withdrawal of Soviet military forces from several countries throughout Eastern Europe. Reforms were accompanied by improved relations between the United States and the Soviet Union, culminating in the Intermediate Nuclear Forces (INF) Treaty, which removed all intermediate range nuclear missiles from Europe. Gorbachev continued to challenge the U. S. leadership in the arena of arms control by announcing in a speech before the United Nations on December 7, 1988, that the Soviet Union's conventional force withdrawals from Eastern Europe would proceed unilaterally.[10] As these concessions took place, progress on the START treaty continued, when the Soviet delegation dropped its demand that reductions in strategic nuclear forces be linked to satisfactory completion of a Defense and Space Treaty.[11]

Although the world seemed to breathe a collective sigh of relief at these developments, other reactions were mixed. Some observers, like Caspar Weinberger and Representative Les Aspin, contended that the United States should welcome these proposals, but keep up its guard, and be as vigilant as ever about the Soviet threat.[12] Others, including Hans Bethe, concluded that Gorbachev represented an unprecedented opportunity to negotiate nuclear disarmament, and argued that the United States should move ahead quickly before the opportunity disappeared.[13] Officials in the Bush administration initially decided to take Weinberger and Aspin's advice by tempering their celebration with caution. In April, 1989, Secretary of State, James Baker, expressed this view, claiming:

These are reasons to be hopeful. But realism requires us to be prudent. The jury is still out on whether the process of reform will succeed. The Soviet Union remains a heavily armed superpower. While its rhetoric is different, the force structure and policies that support far-reaching interests and clients have not yet changed commensurately.[14]

Bush concurred, arguing that although "we are approaching the conclusion of a historic postwar struggle" between the competing visions of "tyranny and conflict and the one of democracy and freedom," the Soviet Union still possessed a vast military arsenal that necessitated caution on the part of the United States.[15]

But as the Berlin Wall collapsed both figuratively and literally in 1989, even administration officials began to acknowledge that the world indeed had changed, and that the threat to national security posed by the Soviet Union was diminishing. In October, 1990, Baker proclaimed:

The epoch of the Cold War is over. Any lingering doubts have been dispelled by the events of the past month. The Cold War in Europe ended quietly in New York on October 1: Foreign Minister Shevardnadze and I joined with our German, British, and French colleagues in signing away the rights of World War II victors, recognizing a new united Germany and the trust among former adversaries that made it possible.[16]

This official end to the Cold War portended changes for SDI as well, as program director Cooper noted, "The world is changing. The Berlin Wall is down. It's not going to go back up."[17] Unfortunately for SDI advocates, these changing world conditions translated into trouble for the program in Congress, as concern over the rising federal budget deficit overshadowed the previous concerns about the Soviet threat.

In Congressional debates over the Bush administration's fiscal year 1991 budget requests, these hesitations to proceed with SDI in full force were evident. In August, 1990, the Senate voted to cut $1 billion from Bush's $4.7 billion proposed budget for SDI, citing the fiscal difficulties facing the nation. "Brilliant pebbles," a new technological development consisting of thousands of small space-based projectiles with powerful computers and sensors on board to direct them to their targets, was proposed in 1988 as a cost saving measure. Although High Frontier, a private lobbying group favoring SDI deployment, estimated the cost of brilliant pebbles at $20 billion, a significant savings over earlier conceptions of potential SDI systems, it was met with Congressional opposition.[18] Senator Sam Nunn, for example, Chair of the Senate Armed Services Committee, criticized the Pentagon for what he perceived to be fiscal irresponsibility. He argued, "No one can tell you where the money's coming from and yet they're charging straight ahead," and that Congress hadn't received "one clue from anybody in his [Bush's] administration" on how to pay for the brilliant pebbles concept.[19] In many ways, this Congressional opposition to SDI funding echoed the debate during the Reagan administration's efforts to secure budgetary support for the program. In the previous chapter, I argued that SDI acquired significant bureaucratic and rhetorical momentum through what I called a "rhetoric of research," in that technological uncertainty became a call for more research and more funding, rather than caution. These same themes were illustrated in a 1989 hearing before the House Subcommittee on Legislation and National Security of the Committee on Government Operations. Lt. General George L. Monahan, testifying on behalf of the SDI Organization, stated that the costs of phase two or three of an SDI system could not be estimated because program officials did not know what those phases would look like, given the changing nature of international security risks.[20] Representative Barbara Boxer vehemently objected to this view, arguing that Congress needed complete cost estimates up front to avoid getting "sucked in" with no way to stop SDI at a future time.[21]

These voices of Congressional opposition to SDI in a time of budget austerity coalesced, and the result was that funding for the program in fiscal year 1991 was cut to $2.9 billion, the lowest level of budgetary support for SDI since 1986.[22] The reasons for this cutback seemed clear; with the end of the Cold War, and the diminishing Soviet threat it represented, brilliant pebbles, and Reagan's grand vision of SDI, was perceived as "a technology in search of a mission."[23]

Even though the dramatic changes in the international scene created rhetorical difficulties for SDI advocates in the late 1980s, ironically, they also created important rhetorical opportunities for the Bush administration to forge a new vision of America's role in the world, one grounded in the sense of destiny and mission associated with symbolic constructions of U. S. history. The end of the Cold War represented proof that the United States and its NATO allies, through vigilance, strength, determination, and patience, had "won" the struggle against communist expansion, and had rightfully earned their place as the dominant military and economic powers in the world arena. Simultaneously, this "victory" offered the hope of a transition to a mythic "new world order," in which democracy, free enterprise, and peace would guide the affairs of nations, led by the shining example of the United States. This new order, although full of hopes and dreams for world peace, was also fraught with danger, as the nations of the world struggled to manage a transition to this mythic order. An important element in the time of transition was a willingness to demonstrate a commitment to preserve this new order, before it could be destroyed by aggressive tyrants wishing to take advantage of its struggle to be born. The 1991 war in the Persian Gulf gave Bush the opportunity to demonstrate such a commitment.

The Symbolic Construction of the Persian Gulf War

On August 2, 1990, Iraq invaded Kuwait, setting off a series of events that would capture the attention of the entire world. President George Bush, working in coalition with dozens of countries and the United Nations Security Council, ordered the deployment of U. S. troops to the Middle East, with the stated intention of deterring an Iraqi attack against Saudi Arabia. This military buildup, numerous resolutions in the Security Council authorizing the use of force to eject Iraq from Kuwait, and Congressional approval of such actions led to a war that showcased high technology weapons, dramatically illustrated the threats posed by the proliferation of ballistic missile technology, and reasserted the strength and leadership of the United States in a post-Cold War world. Examining the Bush administration's rhetorical choices in describing and justifying these actions is important because they created a symbolic context for a redefinition of the objectives sought through SDI, and reenacted the rhetorical forms evident in Reagan's pleas for American military strength in a dangerous world.

As I argued earlier, the end of the Cold War in Europe represented a hopeful time for the world, but also a dangerous one. The Bush Administration pointed out both the joy and fear embodied in the changing international scene in its reactions to the Iraqi invasion of Kuwait. Six days after the attack, Bush addressed the nation in a televised speech, claiming, "We're beginning a new era. This new era can be full of promise—an age of freedom; a time of peace for all peoples."[24] But as hopeful as this scene was, it was also potentially dangerous, in that it represented a crucial moment in world history. Baker explained why American actions in this new scene were particularly important, given that they would be historic moves that could define the future for generations of people to come:

> Iraq's unprovoked aggression is a political test of how the post-Cold War world will work. Amidst the revolutions sweeping the globe and the transformation of East-West relations, we stand at a critical juncture in history. The Iraqi invasion of Kuwait is one of the defining moments of a new era—an era full of promise but also one replete with new challenges.[25]

The scene described in this way was indeed a historic one. If future international order hung in the balance, then actions taken in this hopeful yet dangerous scene took on historic proportions as well. Baker specifically identified the threats the world faced in this scene, when he argued that "emerging dangers are lurking before us," including "ethnic and sectarian conflicts" that breed violence, and "misguided leaders," who "are tempted to assert regional dominance before the ground rules of a new order can be accepted."[26] In an address before the United Nations General Assembly, Bush reasserted the historic proportions of this struggle, and linked Saddam Hussein's invasion of Kuwait to an epic battle between the forces of good and evil:

> Two days from now, the world will be watching when the Cold War is formally buried in Berlin. And in this time of testing, a fundamental question must be asked, a question not for any one nation, but for the United Nations. The question is this: Can we

work together in a new partnership of nations? Can the collective strength of the world community, expressed by the United Nations, unite to deter and defeat aggression? Because the Cold War's battle of ideas is not the last epic battle of this century.[27]

The crisis in the Persian Gulf was, therefore, not merely a territorial dispute, but rather a transcendent struggle over *ideas*; a struggle between the values of freedom, peace, and justice, as opposed to tyranny, aggression, and injustice. This epic battle, taking place at a moment of historic, global significance, was described as one of the most important battles ever fought. The rhetorical structure of the Cold War, which was described by Reagan in similar manichean terms, had been transformed to accommodate changing international circumstances. But any epic scene, whether defined in East-West terms or not, requires heroes and villains who do battle for ultimate purposes. The villain in the Persian Gulf War was defined very clearly by the Bush administration, and he was portrayed in savage terms.

Calling upon a sense of history to justify "drawing a line in the sand" was one way in which Bush administration officials communicated the high stakes involved in the Persian Gulf crisis. Having learned lessons from World War II, the United States, they argued, was not going to stand idly by and let a maniacal dictator march through the Middle East. In his address to the nation, Bush called upon this sense of historical understanding to make clear to the American public just how dangerous Saddam Hussein was to world stability:

> But if history teaches us anything, it is that we must resist aggression or it will destroy our freedoms. Appeasement does not work. As was the case in the 1930s, we see in Saddam Hussein an aggressive dictator threatening his neighbors.[28]

Vice President Dan Quayle echoed this sentiment, when he argued that in 1936, a similar challenge faced the world, when "Adolf Hitler...moved German troops into the Rhineland, in open defiance of the treaties of Versailles and Locarno."[29] In the past, when the United States remained aloof to the challenge posed by Hitler, the result was untold destruction and misery, that Bush described as "a horror which embodied hell on Earth."[30]

In this historic time of transition, the world could not afford to make a similar mistake and ignore the invasion of Kuwait.

But the Bush administration did not make only passing references to Adolf Hitler in its defense of troop deployment in Saudi Arabia. Rather, administration officials described in vivid terms the kind of person who would engage in such outrageous behavior, and they explicitly attributed images of brutality, savagery, and evil to Saddam Hussein. Heroes keep their promises; villains do not, and Bush claimed that Saddam was no exception to this rule:

> Only fourteen days ago, Saddam Hussein promised his friends he would not invade Kuwait. And four days ago, he promised the world he would withdraw. And twice we have seen what his promises mean. His promises mean nothing.[31]

Individuals who fail to keep their promises are liars and cannot be trusted. Given the historic proportions of the crisis, the United States had no choice but to use military force to roll back the Iraqi invasion.

Additionally, administration speakers claimed that the aggression committed by Iraq was by no means insignificant, proportionate, or justified. On the contrary, it was perhaps the most violent and destructive aggression the world had ever seen. Bush administration officials described the invasion in such terms, in order to underscore the drastic need for action to rescue Kuwait from the clutches of this evil villain. Bush called the invasion an "outrageous and brutal act of aggression" that illustrated the "raw territorial ambition of Saddam Hussein."[32] He was a "ruthless aggressor," who used "poison gas" on his own people, committed "atrocities," and enlisted "henchmen" in his attempts to "wipe a country off the face of the earth," which Bush claimed was no exaggeration.[33] Administration officials represented Saddam in savage, animalistic terms, claiming that he had "predatory designs," and that he had no qualms about "devour[ing]" and "swallowing whole a peaceful neighbor."[34]

Savages and animals, of course, do not subscribe to "civilized" standards of behavior, and Saddam was characterized as an individual who did not share in such accepted codes of conduct in the international arena. Bush urged the community of civilized nations to "send a signal to Saddam Hussein that the world will not tolerate tyrants who violate every standard of civilized behavior..."[35] He warned Americans that:

> We must not delude ourselves—Iraq's invasion was more than a military attack on tiny Kuwait; it was a ruthless assault on the very essence of international order and civilized ideals.[36]

Symbol using creatures who, as Burke claimed, are goaded by the spirit of hierarchy, use language to structure reality into those above and those below, and Bush's juxtaposition of Saddam's "uncivilized" behavior against that of the historical mission of the United States was no exception. This hierarchical representation was evident in Bush's claim that, "We are the ones who are standing up for civilized values, standing up for a principle that's almost as old as our republic." America and its allies, in other words, were the keepers of civilization, while Saddam Hussein represented metaphorically all those in the uncivilized world, who failed to learn the lessons of the past. Bush illustrated the point in historical terms by describing the beliefs of Franklin Roosevelt and Harry Truman, when those great American leaders faced similar threats to civilization in World War II and Korea.[37]

A "perfect" enemy, which symbolically is required if one is to achieve complete purification of the guilt-ridden symbolic order, is one which is strong and powerful, and has no moral qualms about preying on weak, defenseless victims. Such was the case with Iraq's invasion of Kuwait, according to administration officials. Kuwait was described as "peaceful" and "tiny," possessing a desert of "vast, still beauty" which "was fouled by the stench of diesel and the roar of steel tanks" on the day of the invasion.[38] Although daunted by the dangers facing them, the Kuwaiti people, fighting against tragedy, trauma and brutality, "are fighting back heroically...[through] an indigenous Kuwaiti resistance...[which] carries on the struggle against Iraqi aggression from inside Kuwait."[39]

This heroic imagery of a tiny nation facing great odds in its struggle for independence was contrasted with Iraq, which was depicted as a powerful nation desiring more destructive technology for its awesome military machine. Bush claimed that Iraq "is already a rich and powerful country...[with] the fourth largest military in the world."[40] But this military might apparently was not enough for Saddam, who had even more ominous designs. As Vice President Dan Quayle put it:

> Saddam's ambitions are not confined to Kuwait. Rather, his goal is to dominate the Persian Gulf region and use its vast wealth to become the greatest Arab hero of modern times, the leader of a new Arab superpower.... And, of course, the prospect of Saddam Hussein strutting across the world stage at the head of a malevolent global power, armed to the teeth with weapons of mass destruction, and controlling a large portion of the world's energy supplies, is something no sane person would welcome.[41]

Given the solidification of its military and political hegemony with the demise of the Cold War, and goaded by the spirit of hierarchy, the United States could not stand by and allow this "malevolent" Arab power to turn into a superpower. As Quayle's discourse suggested by implication, only the insane would embrace such a development.

The invasion of Kuwait represented to administration officials evidence of the hopeful, but dangerous, epic scene facing the world at the close of the Cold War. The villain operating in that scene, however, came to represent metaphorically the dangers inherent in an even larger scene, both in space and in time. The *future* threats posed by the proliferation of nuclear, chemical, and biological weapons, coupled with ballistic missile delivery systems to carry them to distant lands, were symbolically depicted in the *present* through the character of Saddam Hussein. The epic victory of the forces of good over the forces of evil represented both a temporal and spatial transcendence over the dangerous scene, characterized as a "new world order" in which peace, prosperity, and justice would reign. This attempt at transcendence through the dimensions of both time and space were evident in several statements by administration officials during the Persian Gulf War.

Saddam Hussein's invasion of Kuwait was described as an example of past behavior, a throwback to an ancient time rendered irrelevant with the passing of the Cold War. Baker described this regression to the past, when he argued, "The rest of the world is trying to go forward with the 1990s. But Saddam Hussein is trying to drag us all back into the 1930s."[42] He further explained the temporal dimension of the epic scene when he stated:

The line in the sands of Arabia is also a line in *time*. By crossing into Kuwait, Saddam Hussein took a dangerous step back into history[43] (emphasis mine).

In Bush's address to the United Nations, this characterization of the invasion as a backward-looking act was coupled with metaphors of light and dark, representing good and evil. He argued:

> Today, the regime stands isolated and out of step with the times, separated from the civilized world, not by space but by centuries. Iraq's unprovoked aggression is a throwback to another era, a dark relic from a dark time.[44]

The dark, dangerous days of the past were placed in stark contrast to the bright, hopeful days of the future, in which weapons of mass destruction are banished from the Earth, and the world is united in a historic quest for a lasting peace. Bush placed hope for such a future in the United Nations, when he claimed:

> The United Nations can help bring about a new day, a day when these kinds of terrible [chemical] weapons, and the terrible despots who would use them, are both a thing of the past. It is in our hands to leave these dark machines behind, in the Dark Ages where they belong, and to press forward to cap a historic movement toward a new world order and a long era of peace.[45]

This futuristic dream would only come about, however, if the nations of the world acted in the *present* to ensure the survival of this new world order. Refusing to meet Iraq's aggression with determination and commitment would spell doom for this hopeful vision of a peaceful future. Bush explicitly linked the future to the present by arguing:

> This is precisely why the *present* aggression in the gulf is a menace not only to one region's security but to the entire world's vision of our *future*. It threatens to turn the dream of a new international order into a grim nightmare of anarchy in which the law of the jungle supplants the law of nations (emphasis mine).[46]

This vision of a new world order, however, was to be transcendent not only in time, but also in space. The struggle for the liberation of Kuwait represented an uphill climb, one that would ensure that the nations of the world reached a plateau of shining peace, untouched by the ravages of the dark nightmarish past. This transcendent vision, with its merger of time and space, culminated in the conclusion of Bush's speech, when he proclaimed:

> The world must know and understand: From this hour, from this day, from this hall, we step forth with a new sense of purpose, a new sense of possibilities. We stand together, prepared to swim upstream, to march uphill, to tackle the tough challenges as they come—not only as the United Nations, but as the nations of the world united. And so let it be said of the final decade of the 20th century: This was a time when humankind came into its own, when we emerged from the grit and the smoke of the industrial age to bring about a revolution of the spirit and the mind and began a journey into a new day, a new age, and a new partnership of nations.[47]

Bush's transcendent vision of a new world order, then was similar in symbolic form to Reagan's vision of the Strategic Defense Initiative. According to Reagan, SDI would lift humanity above the dangerous material conditions inherent in the Cold War through the promising technology of the future. Through patience and perseverance, the United States would someday be free from the threat of nuclear war, if only it would put its faith in the historically proven tools of American technological ingenuity. Once achieved, this defensive system would provide the nation with the ability to transcend the nuclear age and return to a state of pre-nuclear innocence. Bush's vision made a similar promise, that through the strength of American leadership in a United Nations unfettered by the political disputes of the Cold War, the world would rise up into a future full of hope and peace. The symbolic elements of this vision, as revealed in the administration's discourse during the Persian Gulf War, have important implications for the Strategic Defense Initiative in its newest form, Global Protection Against Limited Strikes (GPALS).

SDI in the Post-Cold War World

As I argued earlier, the demise of the Cold War presented a difficult rhetorical challenge for the Bush administration in its attempts to justify continuation of research and development for the Strategic Defense Initiative. Once the Soviet threat abated, there seemed to be little reason to pursue a defensive system to intercept intercontinental ballistic missiles in space. But the post-Cold War international scene, as described by administration speakers, was a time of hope, but also danger. One of the most significant threats to international stability in the time of transition, they claimed, was the proliferation of weapons of mass destruction and sophisticated ballistic missile delivery systems.

The United States was always concerned about nuclear proliferation, as illustrated by its participation in international efforts to prevent the spread of nuclear technologies, such as the Nuclear Proliferation Treaty. But the end of the Cold War seemed to heighten the fears associated with proliferation, as it became clear that the bipolar structure of U. S.–Soviet relations, coupled with dual spheres of interest all around the world, would no longer serve to deter would-be nuclear powers from starting regional wars that could escalate to the superpower level. Baker pointed to the risks posed by nuclear, chemical, and biological weapons proliferation, when he argued that the United States and the Soviet Union should address "new global dangers, such as missile proliferation, and an old problem—chemical warfare—that unfortunately has been revived."[48] Referring to the collapse of the bipolar international structure, he argued that the United States must prepare for an emerging multipolar world, both in military and economic terms.[49] The stakes in this time of transition were high, and proliferation was described as "perhaps the greatest security challenge of the 1990s."[50]

The dimensions of this emerging threat to world stability were outlined by a Central Intelligence Agency report, which concluded that by the year 2000 fifteen additional nations would acquire ballistic missile technologies, bringing the total number of countries possessing advanced warhead delivery systems to twenty-four worldwide.[51] An awareness of the dangers of ballistic missile proliferation and hopes that SDI technologies could alleviate these threats, however, did not begin with the Patriot's performance in the Gulf War. As early as 1989, Senator Sam Nunn urged Congress to fund an Accidental Launch Protection System (ALPS) to shield the United States in the event of unauthorized launches of ballistic missiles, or even deliberate attacks by emerging nuclear powers.[52] Given a new-found appreciation for these future threats to national security, SDI Director, Henry Cooper proposed that the program be modified to meet such threats, rather than an all-out attack from the Soviet Union.[53]

The Persian Gulf War, however, was an important illustration of the threat posed by ballistic missile proliferation, and served to solidify for many the need to redirect the SDI program toward these more limited objectives. Iraq's possession and use of Scud missiles against Israel and Saudi Arabia dramatically demonstrated the nature of the ballistic missile threat. Television viewers around the world saw with their own eyes live coverage of Scud attacks, frightened Israelis, journalists struggling to put on gas masks, and most importantly, Patriot anti-missile missiles intercepting Scuds in flight, creating fiery explosions in the night sky. Viewers also watched in horror as a Scud destroyed military barracks in northern Saudi Arabia, killing scores of American servicemen and women, and feared that the next missile might carry a chemical warhead. Given such dramatic images of the dangers of proliferation, it would seem that a limited version of SDI, modeled after the Patriot, would be a prudent investment.

Secretary of Defense, Dick Cheney was one of many who expressed this view. He argued:

> If there was ever evidence that supported the notion for aggressively going forward with the [SDI] program, it would seem to me it was watching those Scuds fly at Tel Aviv and Riyadh.[54]

Kenneth Adelman, former director of the Arms Control and Disarmament Agency in the Reagan administration, pointed out how the Persian Gulf War changed public perceptions of SDI, when he stated, "How ironic that the most maligned weapons of the 1980s have become the most marvelous weapons of 1991."[55] In an emphatic plea for continued SDI research, the editorial board of the *Wall Street Journal* contended that the Scud interceptions illustrated the soundness of the moral principle originally envisioned by Reagan in his SDI discourse:

> The strategic defense debate ended about 3 a.m. last Friday, Saudi Arabia time. That's when the now-famous Patriot system

slammed into a Scud missile, the first of many interceptions now occurring daily. Yes, the Patriot isn't full-blown "Star Wars." But the principle of intercepting missiles before they hit civilians is what most SDI supporters, including us, have been promoting all along.[56]

Supporters of the Strategic Defense Initiative recognized, however, that the Iraqi Scud missiles were crude and relatively ineffective weapons and that future ballistic missile threats would be significantly more deadly and ominous. Keith Payne voiced this sentiment, when he argued that the Scud attacks during the Gulf War "offer only a modest taste of the threat likely to be posed by ballistic missiles" in the near future.[57] With these warnings in mind, Bush officially announced the redirection of SDI towards these dangers in his 1991 State of the Union Address, when he called upon technological optimism, and proclaimed:

Now, with remarkable technological advances like the Patriot missile, we can defend against ballistic missile attacks aimed at innocent civilians. Looking forward, I have directed that the SDI program be refocused on providing protection from limited ballistic missile strikes—whatever their source. Let us pursue an SDI program that can deal with any future threat to the United States, to our forces overseas, and to our friends and allies.[58]

Although the Bush administration's rhetorical posture on GPALS is just emerging, some conclusions about it can be drawn, given the symbolic context created by the end of the Cold War, the administration's discourse during the Gulf War, and some early representations of GPALS from administration officials and observers alike. Given these contextual factors, I shall argue that the emerging symbolic construction of GPALS is expressed in colonizing discursive forms, in which the hegemonic position of the United States, in military, political, economic, and ideological terms, is maintained and strengthened. Savage images of Saddam Hussein, coupled with fears about ballistic missile proliferation combine to create a discursive environment that solidifies and reenacts in discourse the historical exploitation of the "South" by the "North," and transforms the representations of the East-West conflict into the North-South arena.

In a recent essay, Edward W. Said argued that much discourse about so-called "Third World" nations reproduces and reinforces the ideology of colonialism, in that linguistic practices that represent the colonized have ideological and material consequences.[59] He claimed that the phrase "Third World" originated as a way to speak about those nations historically colonized by hegemonic powers, such as Great Britain, Spain, Portugal, Holland, France, and the United States.[60] The colonized, he argued, are not merely a historical group that won independence through struggle and strife, but are newly independent states who still find themselves "occupied" by more powerful nations in a variety of ways. One way in which the experience of colonization continues is through the enduring material effects of occupation. Said argued:

> To have been colonized was a fate with lasting, indeed grotesquely unfair results, especially after national independence had been achieved. Poverty, dependency, underdevelopment, various pathologies of power and corruption, plus of course notable achievements in war, literacy, economic development: this mix of characteristics designated the colonized people who had freed themselves on one level but who remained victims of their past on another.[61]

According to Said, discourse represents colonized peoples by reinforcing these material results of colonization and allowing them to be perpetuated, thus preserving the hegemony of the colonizers. In a way, this is similar to Burke's claim that human beings use language, but language also uses us; words employed to "name" a situation, a group, an individual, or a thing imply an attitude, which Burke claimed is an incipient act. Describing a country as "underdeveloped" implies an ideal of development represented, of course, by the industrial capitalism of the North. A "Third World" nation is two notches below "First World" countries on a hierarchy of international prestige. In other words, how language represents an oppressed group has important consequences for how individuals and societies act toward that group. Said explained the implications of discursive practices in defining the colonized:

> Thus the status of colonized people has been fixed in zones of dependency and peripherality, stigmatized in the designation of

underdeveloped, less-developed, developing states, ruled by a superior, developed, or metropolitan colonizer...[62]

Abdul Jan Mohamed explicitly drew the connection between "discursive" and "material" colonization, arguing that symbolic representations of colonized peoples actualize violence in the symbolic realm that is as real and consequential as physical violence. He argued:

> the discursive practices do to the symbolic, linguistic presence of the native what the material practices do to his physical presence; the writer commodifies him so that he can be exploited more efficiently by the administrator, who, of course, obliges by returning the favor in kind.[63]

Oppressed in both the symbolic and material realms, colonized groups find themselves without a voice in the ongoing international dialogue. In a world in which "superpowers" exert a controlling influence in the global arena, as illustrated by the veto power granted to nuclear armed nations in the United Nations Security Council, those without power attempt to be heard in many ways. One way in which such groups attempt to find a voice, Said argued, is through the acquisition of arms. He claimed that the colonized "are driven increasingly to more and more desperate remedies," and many "decide that only their own military force will compel Paris or London to take them seriously as interlocutors." Only by making "enough noise," are these groups acknowledged and invited into a dialogue with the powerful.[64] Nuclear, chemical, and biological weapons proliferation, although frightening to contemplate, can be read as an attempt by historically oppressed nations to assert their presence and influence in the international scene, to be "taken seriously" by the dominant global powers. With the Gulf War now behind us, it is perhaps ironic that in one of Said's most influential works, he argued that Western conceptions and characterizations of Arab nations in particular are replete with discursive forms that reproduce the ideology of colonialism.[65]

Given my premise that language shapes reality, in that an understanding of the material world is constructed through the use of symbols, such representations of historically oppressed groups have real and significant consequences. If "Third World" enemies are portrayed as uncivilized, savage brutes with animalistic tendencies, it is easier to justify enslaving them, going to war against them, or killing them without guilt. An examination of discourse advocating Bush's GPALS program, read in the context of the war in the Persian Gulf, illustrates how it functions to reproduce the ideology of colonialism in a variety of ways.

GPALS, as described by Bush, is designed to develop and deploy effective defenses against limited ballistic missile attacks, regardless of the source of those attacks. Whether launched by accident or design, from nuclear armed terrorist groups or new nuclear powers, GPALS would destroy the incoming missiles before they had a chance to reach their targets. In describing the groups or nations that soon could acquire a ballistic missile capability, administration officials and GPALS advocates portray them as unstable, irrational, uncivilized, and hostile, thereby reifying the ideology of colonialism and solidifying U. S. hegemony.

In commenting on the risks posed by nuclear proliferation, Secretary of Defense Cheney claimed that in the near future, "*second class* powers will become first class threats...." (emphasis mine).[66] Similarly, in his defense of Bush's GPALS program, Payne contended that in the future, "third parties" (as opposed to "first" or "second" parties), could threaten the United States with ballistic missiles.[67] The implication is that these emerging nuclear powers are second or third class citizens (i.e. "Third World" nations), and that they are somehow lower on the global hierarchy than the United States. In contrast, during the Gulf War, the United States was placed directly at the top of this hierarchy, when Baker described it as "the finest and greatest country in the world," and Bush proclaimed, "Among the nations of the world, only the United States of America" has the moral leadership necessary for victory, that "We are the only nation on this Earth that could assemble the forces of peace," and that leadership and strength "made America the beacon of freedom in a searching world."[68]

In addition to occupying a low-status position in the hierarchical order, nations attempting to acquire weapons of mass destruction are represented as unstable and even irrational, and, therefore, cannot be trusted with dangerous technology like nuclear armed ballistic missiles. Reproducing the manichean representations of Saddam Hussein during the Persian Gulf War, Payne argued that the list of countries with the potential for proliferation includes "bellicose countries hostile to the United States, its allies, and friends," and "autocratic regimes capable of reckless and possibly irrational acts of aggression."[69] As I demonstrated earlier, Iraq was described in similar terms during the Persian Gulf War, calling forth images of ruthless and reckless aggression, brutality, bellicosity, and hostility. In this way, the dualistic rhetorical structure of the Cold War, which described the Soviet Union as hostile, ruthless, and brutal, has been transferred into a new era, one in which the world is struggling to manage a dangerous transition to a multipolar world.

The enemies faced in this new era, however, seem even more dangerous than the Soviets, in that they are portrayed not only as hostile and brutal, but also irrational, unstable, uncivilized, and backward. Jan Mohamed argued that discourse recreating the manichean allegory, in which dualistic structures of meaning representing good and evil do battle, is a central feature of colonialist cognitive frameworks and symbolic forms. Dualisms such as good-evil, white-black, superior-inferior, and civilized-savage reinforce patterns of thought that justify and perpetuate the colonialist ideology.[70] Seen in the context of the Gulf War, the discourse of GPALS advocates serves this function. During the war, Saddam Hussein's brutal, unprovoked invasion of Kuwait was presented as evidence for the claim that he was "uncivilized," and violated established international rules of civilized conduct. Similarly, the invasion was portrayed as a backward-looking act, one that brought the world back into the "dark ages," when nations preyed on one another with impunity. Saddam Hussein was described as a savage, even sub-human, as he "devoured and swallowed whole" a nation upon which he had "predatory designs." In colonialist terms, uncivilized, backwards, savage brutes like those purported to be found in Africa, Asia, and the "New World," in past centuries, needed to be civilized by the "advanced" nations.

Payne pointed to what he saw as some of the "uncivilized" characteristics of newly emerging nuclear powers, when he claimed:

> Countries with embryonic ballistic missile forces are likely to lack the technical safeguards and practical experience necessary to ensure that missiles cannot be launched without proper authorization, or as a result of mechanical malfunctions or human error.[71]

These countries, "embryonic" both in terms of technical safeguards and industrial development, therefore, have not "advanced" to the point where they have the skill, technical resources, and "practical" experience to effectively manage and control dangerous new weapons systems. Unlike the United States in 1945, which in Payne's view apparently *did* have practical experience with nuclear weapons, these countries cannot be trusted with such destructive power. Images of savagery, coupled with those of uncivilized behavior combine to create rhetorically compelling enemies, against which the United States must protect itself and its allies. As John Pike claimed:

[SDI proponents] have seized upon something scarier than an accidental launch, more evil than a rogue submarine commander, and roughly as odious as nuclear holocaust: Col. Muammar Qaddafi [or Saddam Hussein]. They argue that Star Wars is America's only hope in a world of steadily proliferating long-range ballistic missiles and increasingly crazy dictators such as Qaddafi and the Ayatollah Khomeini.[72]

In this view, a global scene characterized by the proliferation of weapons of mass destruction and advanced delivery systems is a dangerous one, not only due to the uncivilized nature of emerging powers, but also because it would represent a direct challenge to the dominant military position occupied by the United States at the end of the Cold War. This position was illustrated earlier in Quayle's claim that Saddam was striving to be the leader of a "malevolent Arab superpower," one that could control world affairs through its domination of the Persian Gulf region and its possession of weapons of mass destruction. Payne contended that nuclear proliferation would threaten U. S. national security interests by "imposing significant constraints" on future foreign policy options, and that "in considering power projection alternatives, U. S. leaders would have to calculate the possibility of Third Party ballistic missile strikes...."[73] In other words, the freedom of action the United States has by virtue of its awesome military force would be challenged by nuclear proliferation. Its position as the dominant world military power, which grants it the hegemonic ability to "project its power" all around the world, would be threatened. The mere possession of nuclear weapons and delivery systems by "Third World" nations, therefore, threatens to remove the United States from its position at the top of the global hierarchy. As Payne argued:

> In short, merely by acquiring long-range ballistic missiles, Third Parties could *gain international prestige,* constrain U. S. diplomacy, undermine U. S. security guarantees, and deter U. S. and allied power projection into local conflicts (emphasis mine).[74]

Pursuing and deploying GPALS, however, would allow the United States to recapture its freedom of action in local conflicts, and, thereby, maintain its position of superiority in world affairs. Such a defensive system, in fact, if deployed in outer space through the technology of brilliant pebbles, would provide the United States with an ability to maintain "a distant presence" in remote regions, which would be more politically acceptable to its allies than troop deployment.[75] In an ironic but powerful way, GPALS would allow the United States to "be present" in regional conflicts, without being materially present, thus, avoiding the physical and political risks associated with "power projection" or colonial occupation.

With the deployment of GPALS, the United States would, therefore, be a transcendent power, able to pursue its foreign policies from afar, and, with help from space based defensive systems, would be physically transcendent above material concerns. This vision of GPALS, together with a "new world order" that is both spatially and temporally transcendent, represents a compelling symbolic response to the dangerous international scene—one which reassures Americans that although the world is changing rapidly, the United States will maintain its position as the "shining city on a hill." No longer bound by the deterministic impulses of a dangerous scene that is beyond human control, the United States, through its faith in technology and its role as a global leader, will be able to finally fulfill its ultimate mission to free the world from injustice and oppression. Although similar in form to Reagan's conception of a post-SDI world, Bush's vision has the added rhetorical benefit of a stunning victory in the Persian Gulf War, which dramatically illustrated the strength and promise of American power, technology, and values.

Conclusion

The president of the United States, given the Constitutional authority to conduct foreign relations, has great influence over debates concerning national security issues. The Strategic Defense Initiative provides a compelling example of the power of the president and the executive branch of the federal government to define the national debate over controversial defense issues. How is presidential power manifested symbolically and rhetorically? What implications does it have for the study of American foreign policy? How can the study of discursive forms and symbolic representations add to our understanding of foreign policy? In the final chapter, I will suggest answers to these questions.

As technology progresses, and as the social, political, and ecological problems associated with technology continue to appear, decision makers in the United States and abroad are faced with complex and threatening problems that demand solutions. Environmental pollution, depletion of the ozone layer, climatic changes due to the burning of fossil fuels, deforestation, and many other pressing global problems have at least one thing in common; they are all partially caused by the advances in technology that ironically have also improved the quality of life for millions of people worldwide.

In an age characterized simultaneously by technological promise and catastrophe, how can the age old traditions of public deliberation and debate contribute to finding solutions to problems and implementing policies? The SDI debate illustrates the difficulties involved in creating a national dialogue concerning emerging technologies. The next chapter asks how public argument can function in an era dominated by technology.

6.

Public Debate in an
Age of Strategic Defense

THE STRATEGIC DEFENSE INITIATIVE is symbolically powerful for many reasons. President Ronald Reagan identified SDI with traditional American concepts of virtue, destiny, and mission, and he linked the program to the American tradition of conquering new frontiers. By doing so, Reagan united his supporters with important traditions in American history. As symbolically constructed by Reagan, SDI subverted the rhetorical appeal of the peace movement, as embodied in the nuclear freeze proposal. Touted as a way to render nuclear missiles obsolete, SDI seemed to offer a more promising solution to the nuclear arms race than did the nuclear freeze. The Reagan administration's SDI discourse created a niche for the program whereby it was insulated from strong criticism, but, simultaneously, was rhetorically self-perpetuating. President George Bush's reformulation of SDI toward security threats posed by nuclear proliferation, in conjunction with the representations of Saddam Hussein as a savage, uncivilized tyrant, identified the program with notions of American superiority and strength in a changing international scene. Given these conclusions about SDI, it is important to consider some of their broader implications.

In this chapter, I will elaborate upon the role of language and discursive practices in foreign policy, the institutional and symbolic powers of the presidency, the role of technology in public debate, and the implications of these factors on the study of U. S. foreign policy. In doing so, I will argue that all foreign policy is discursively constructed, and that it serves to silence voices of opposition in many ways. When foreign policy is embodied in technological developments, as in the case of SDI, it is perhaps even more difficult to challenge, given the historical contextualiza-

115

tion of technology in the sense of America's destiny. Issues concerning foreign relations are inevitably shielded from close public scrutiny due to the need for secrecy, the sensitive and complicated nature of the issues, and the power vested in the Executive branch of the federal government to make foreign policy. Public debate over an issue like SDI, therefore, is shaped and constrained by these factors. Technological issues, on the other hand, are shielded from public debate due to the cult of expertise surrounding technology, the specialized language of technicians, and the sense of awe and wonder concerning technology. Identifying how each of these constraints operates in a single controversy can help guide future research in the area of foreign policy discourse and the role of public debate in a technological age.

Public Involvement in American Foreign Policy

One of the most important controversies surrounding the American system of governance is the issue of who should control foreign policy. Should the President, the constitutionally designated Commander-in-Chief of the armed forces, take primary responsibility for directing America's relations with foreign governments? Should Congress, with its control of the purse strings of government, ultimately be responsible for questions of foreign policy? Or should citizens, from whom power is derived in classical democratic theory, determine the course of America's relations with the rest of the world? These questions have plagued theorists of government, practicing politicians, historians, and even rhetorical scholars for centuries.

The romantic and perhaps naive answer to this question is that "the people" reign sovereign over all matters, foreign and domestic. The notion that ordinary citizens in the United States influence foreign policy, and are qualified to do so, is not an idea widely shared among those concerned with the practice of American foreign policy. Even some of the founders of the Constitution were opposed to public control of foreign policy. Alexander Hamilton and James Madison, commenting on the drafting of the U.S. Constitution, argued that matters of foreign relations were too complex and delicate to leave to the emotional, unstable, and incoherent views of the masses of people.[1] While visiting the young nation decades later,

Alexis de Tocqueville concluded that American democracy was a "decidedly inferior" method for foreign policy decision making.[2]

In more recent times, theorists of international relations have argued that mass public opinion is unstable and, therefore, dangerous if given the power to influence foreign policy. Walter Lippman argued, for example, that "the unhappy truth is that the prevailing public opinion [concerning world affairs] has been destructively wrong at critical junctures."[3] Hans Morgenthau claimed that the public was ill-equipped epistemologically for foreign policy decision making. He wrote, "The kind of thinking required for the successful conduct of foreign policy must at times be diametrically opposed to the kind of consideration by which the masses and their representatives are likely to be moved."[4] During the Cold War, these ideas gradually became institutionalized in the foreign policy bureaucracy, as increasing emphasis was placed on training, expertise, and crisis management skills of the type that were not readily available to ordinary American citizens.[5]

As the institutionalization of expertise flourished in the foreign policy decision making community, scholars in the field of international relations began to recognize that the romantic myth of public involvement in foreign policy had dissolved. In his research concerning the role of public opinion and attitudes in the conduct of American foreign policy, Gabriel Almond argued that when scholars assume that the people are inherently wise, just, and powerful in a democracy, a "morally satisfying demagogy" is upheld over the interests of the advancement of knowledge.[6] Additionally, in 1969, Gabriel Kolko contended:

> The theory of public attitudes as the fount of the decision-making process reinforces a democratic theory of legitimacy, which, for reasons of sentimental tradition at home and ideological warfare abroad, is a useful social myth. But the close and serious student of modern American foreign relations will rarely, if ever, find an instance of an important decision made with any reference to the alleged general public desires or opinions.[7]

One could argue, however, that the Vietnam War and the public activism against it forever shattered the myth of an impotent public. A case can be made for the conclusion that public opposition and vocal protests against the war eventually led to withdrawal from Southeast Asia. Although some students of the war have come to this conclusion, Leslie Gelb and Richard Betts persuasively argued that those who wanted to end the war through withdrawal were consistently outnumbered by those who wanted to end the war through escalation. They contended that American actions in the Vietnam War are best explained by the conclusion that the decisions made were compromises between these two alternatives, compromises that neither completely satisfied nor alienated any one group.[8]

The romantic view of public control over foreign policy may be accurate to a certain extent. It can be argued that elected officials feel compelled to avoid supporting policies that are unpopular with voters. Robert P. Newman argued, for example, that domestic public concern over the "fall" of China to communism constrained policy choices to such a degree that decision makers were compelled to deeper involvement in the Vietnam War two decades later.[9] From this perspective, public opinion can influence foreign policy, but only in a general and diffuse way. My concern here is with the apparent lack of public debate over substantive issues in American foreign policy. Public voices, especially those in opposition to the status quo, simply do not exert real and powerful substantive influence in the formulation of foreign policy. One important function of undertaking a critical analysis of U. S. foreign policy, I believe, is to attempt to open a space for alternative viewpoints and interpretations, to challenge the power and authority of dominant understandings of foreign policy.

Given my analysis of the symbolic construction of the Strategic Defense Initiative, I agree with those who conclude that the foreign affairs discourse of technical and governmental voices so dominate the public space that ordinary American citizens are left with no effective oppositional voice.[10] But what is it about foreign policy discourse per se that constrains opposing voices? Examining the symbolic and institutional powers of the presidency, combined with the inherent complexity of international relations in the 20th century, can provide one answer to this question. Focusing on the symbolic manifestations of presidential power can lead scholars toward approaches that may prove fruitful in helping to understand the role that language and symbols play in American foreign policy.

Complexity and Presidential Power
in Foreign Policy

As the end of the twentieth century approaches, nations are becoming increasingly interdependent in the realms of economics, communications, politics, and defense. The fact that weapons of mass destruction can deliver devastation hundreds of times more powerful than Hiroshima halfway around the globe, in only a matter of minutes, confirms that the world is undoubtedly much smaller than it was forty years ago. These same military capabilities, unfortunately, also serve to make the management of world affairs incredibly complex. Alliances, the global balance of power, Third World instability, nuclear proliferation, treaty obligations, unspoken commitments, and many other factors must be considered when a nation, especially a nuclear-armed superpower, contemplates a change in its foreign policy. As the complexity of world affairs increases, so do the stakes involved in decision making. Even a slight miscalculation concerning an adversary's likely response to a change in policy, especially in a time of tension and crisis, can set off a chain of events that may be difficult to control. In such a time of crisis, competing interests and policies require delicate balancing and assessment.

Given such complexity and risk, it is not difficult to understand why ordinary citizens have been excluded from foreign policy decision making, through both official government secrecy and the cult of expertise. In the case of nuclear weapons policy in particular, complex interrelationships between concepts of deterrence, weapons capabilities, strategic doctrine, and diplomatic objectives provide defense intellectuals and specialists with the power to set the national nuclear agenda.[11] Whether or not ordinary citizens are capable of understanding and passing good judgment on such complex problems is not the issue.[12] Rather, my point is that those in positions of power *perceive* that the public is incapable of making the delicate judgments necessary for an effective and safe foreign policy. In other words, the issue is one of power; those with the expertise, the access to information, and the institutional capability decide what foreign policy information is released to the public and what information is officially classified as secret. Those who possess the institutional power also come to possess the discursive power to define situations, choose alternatives, and control the foreign policy pseudo-debate. Those without access to institutional power are also without information and, consequently, left subject to the dictates of the elite cadre of decision makers.

This power literally to control the symbolic arsenal is not the only factor that should concern scholars of foreign policy discourse. An even more potent source of institutional and symbolic power lies in the office of the presidency. Any critic of foreign policy must understand the ways in which the symbolic trappings of the presidency combine with the institutional powers of the office to shape symbolic constructions of foreign policy.

The institutional powers of the president to shape foreign policy are immense. The Constitution of the United States provides that the president is the Commander-in-Chief of the armed forces and that as such he or she has ultimate responsibility for national defense. Congress has the right and responsibility to check the president's power in this arena, and, at times, Congress can frustrate the executive's desires. But even the War Powers Act, which was intended to limit presidential power, concedes that the president has the ultimate authority over international affairs. This institutional structure drastically limits the potential for public participation in the formulation of foreign policy. An ordinary citizen has little, if any, influence over what takes place in the innermost chambers of the White House, even in an election year.[13]

More importantly, however, the institutional power vested in the president leads to vast symbolic power as well. The Executive branch of the Federal Government shapes foreign policy through discourse. In other words, the Executive defines and names foreign policy, and, therefore, creates symbolic interpretations of events. Any discursive practice, including the creation of foreign policy, dramatically shapes and constrains the alternative views competing in the symbolic arena. But when coupled with vast institutional, bureaucratic, and economic power, these discursive practices can drown out alternative opposing voices. Such discursive power can be illustrated with examples from the nuclear freeze campaign, and Reagan's discussion of the Strategic Defense Initiative.

I argued in chapter 3 that one factor leading to the rising support for the nuclear freeze movement was the Reagan administration's "loose talk" concerning nuclear warfighting strategies, civil defense, and limited nuclear war scenarios. Although Reagan's policy concerning warfighting options was not substantially different from Carter's, official statements from the Reagan White House used language that was less euphemistic than previous statements. What Carter's advisers referred to as escalatory "options," Caspar Weinberger called "nuclear warfighting." Assuming for the moment that foreign policy discourse somehow is separate from "reality," the substance of Reagan's policy was the same as Carter's; only the language used to describe it publicly had changed.[14] Betts agreed with this assessment, when he argued that the freeze campaign was energized in part by Reagan's belligerent rhetoric, and that "his loose talk about limited nuclear war simply thrust into wider consciousness the reality of what official doctrine has been for over two decades."[15] In other words, *talk* about policy is what matters, not some extra-symbolic "reality" of policy itself.

Betts also argued, however, that the president does not have free rein when it comes to foreign policy. He claimed that the freeze campaign was a case in point, since it illustrated that a massive public uprising could constrain the foreign policy choices of a powerful American president. Upon closer examination, however, Betts' argument only serves to reinforce my claim about the *symbolic* power of the president to define situations. In Betts' words:

> The Executive, however, does not have a free hand. As the recent "freeze" movement suggests, amorphous frustrations can accumulate and, when ignited by *careless official rhetoric that sounds insensitive to nuclear horror,* can hamper the most ambitious elements of administration strategy. (Emphasis mine)[16]

If, in this case, the "official rhetoric" was indeed "careless," then Reagan could have avoided the ignition of amorphous public passions merely by choosing more appropriate language. In other words, the symbolic power still lies with the president. This example merely illustrates that in this particular case, that symbolic power was executed unwisely.

Another example of the power of presidents to dominate foreign policy discourse concerns Reagan's use of metaphor in describing the Strategic Defense Initiative. In chapter 4, I argued that opponents of SDI found themselves in a difficult rhetorical situation. Reagan effectively identified SDI with America's great tradition of excellence and progress in the technological realm and with America's perceived innocence in foreign affairs. One important way in which he accomplished this identification was through the use of metaphor. According to Reagan, SDI was like a roof that would protect a family from rain; it was, in other words, a benign, purely defensive system with the most noble of purposes, protecting children from adversity. The metaphor itself conveyed the innocence and nobility of the project, and opponents had to assume that the government had ignoble and immoral motives if they wished to argue against SDI. In addition, Reagan claimed SDI was like an insurance policy; a prudent, if expensive, investment that protected citizens from risk. In other words, SDI was practical and worth the cost. Opponents of the program would apparently prefer that the nation take its chances with the Soviets, and spend its money on less "practical" matters.

Since the president has the power to name in the realm of foreign affairs, he or she has the power to construct "reality" for domestic audiences when discussing foreign policy. Coupled with the complexity of international relations, the high stakes in the nuclear age, and the institutional power of the presidency, this power to name is highly significant. Given a public that is relatively uninformed about foreign affairs, confused by nuclear issues, sufficiently frightened, and denied access to important classified information, there can be little doubt that a key element in developing a thorough understanding of the discursive practices of U. S. foreign policy lies in the explication of the symbolic powers of the presidency.

Dualism in Foreign Policy Discourse

Given the vast institutional and discursive power to define foreign policy, how is it symbolically constructed? What rhetorical forms are evident in U. S. foreign policy? Discursive forms that describe world events as ultimate struggles between good and evil, such as those enacted by Reagan and Bush in their defenses of SDI, serve to reinforce dualistic structures of meaning. By reducing U. S. foreign policy options to only two choices (good-evil, civilization-savagery), such representations deny the legitimacy of other views that may lie somewhere between the polar extremes. One result is that opposition to policy translates into a form of treason, and support of policy is constructed as the only obvious choice for audiences.

Robert Ivie illustrated the dualistic nature of foreign policy discourse when he argued that presidential justifications for war throughout American history have centered on attributing images of savagery to the enemy. Accounts of atrocities, brute force, enslavement, and irrational savagery abound in such rhetoric, devoid of any sense of subtlety or doubt.[17] In another essay, Ivie focused on Reagan's discourse in particular, and concluded that his rhetorical stance toward the Soviet Union tolerated no ambiguity or uncertainty about Soviet motives.[18] In yet another piece, Ivie contended that U. S. audiences are presented with two starkly opposed views of the Soviet Union. One, the Cold War view, inexorably leads to armageddon, and the other, the idealists' view, offers only pacifism as an alternative response to Soviet tyranny.[19] These studies serve to illustrate that representations of U. S. foreign policy discourse reproduce manichean dualism, with its bipolar structure of meaning. The inevitable nuances and grey areas of foreign relations are disguised by the apparently dualistic choices described by the speakers.

This tendency is illustrated in pro-SDI discourse as well. As I argued in chapter 4, Reagan's version of SDI as a leakproof population defense created symbolic advantages for the program, in that it represented "good" in a material world dominated by "evil." In chapter 5, I demonstrated the importance of Bush's attribution of images of savagery and brutality to Saddam Hussein during and after the Persian Gulf War, in that it allowed the administration to reassert U. S. hegemony through discourse. Students of international relations have commented on a similar historical tendency for American presidents to describe threats to national security in grave terms in order to guarantee public support for policy. Truman's flamboyant rhetoric concerning the global Soviet threat, for example, was necessary to overcome Congressional inertia over the Truman Doctrine's conception of containment. Crusading anti-Soviet rhetoric was necessary to guarantee public support for Cold War policies.[20] Such bipolar rhetorical forms recur in representations of U. S. foreign policy because of their ability to create a sense of order and predictability in a chaotic and confusing international scene. In Burkean terms, the complexity, confusion, high risk, and uncertainty in a dangerous world leads to a loss of faith in the existing international order. Citizens fearful of the consequences of international conflict seek reassurance that the international order is sound and stable, and that the current conceptions of American foreign policy are still functional and appropriate sets of symbols. In such an unstable, risky, and uncertain world, the establishment sects, those with institutional and symbolic power, redefine situations, and attempt to stretch the taken-for-granted meanings embedded in the established order, as Bush adapted the symbolic understandings of the East-West conflict to a post-Cold War world. As the stretching is employed again and again, however, and as it reaches a critical point, the established order appears more and more like a caricature of its former self. Extreme adversity requires an extremely stable and inflexible order, and the most stable order of all is one that is simple, one with little flexibility, one that orders experience clearly and sharply. A dualistic structure of meaning accomplishes these purposes.

Reagan's manichean worldview that portrayed the U. S.–Soviet rivalry as a cosmic battle between the forces of good and the forces of evil, provided the symbolic security and stability needed to make sense of the world in troubled times. And when it became necessary symbolically to sacrifice a scapegoat the most perfect enemy, the ultimate scapegoat, was the one that exhibited all of the evil characteristics of brutality to the utmost. The Soviets, once called by Reagan the focus of evil in the modern world, were in this way the perfect collective scapegoat. Ivie eloquently explained how this logic accounted for U. S.–Soviet relations during the Cold War:

> The public will continue to express uneasiness over the arms race and voice its desire for better relations with the Russians, but it will ultimately respond to the clarion call rather than muddle forever through ambiguities and uncertainties. Even more threatening than the long-term possibility of a nuclear holocaust is the immediate prospect of disorientation and chaos among symbol-using/symbol-misusing animals fraught with the drive for perfection but lacking the convenience of a scapegoat.[21]

One could easily apply this logic to U. S. foreign policy at the end of the Persian Gulf War as well. Rather than muddle through the ambiguities and uncertainties surrounding the war's impact on the future of the Middle East, the Kurdish and Shiite populations in Iraq, and the economic and medical hardship faced by Iraqi civilians, it is easier to focus attention on the stunning victory of the allied forces, and the savage image of Saddam Hussein. If the U. S. represents the forces of good in a dangerous era, it seems only natural that it should retain its place at the top of the global hierarchy of power.

The controversies over the Strategic Defense Initiative and the Gulf War are merely two examples of how foreign policy is constructed discursively in dualistic forms that serve to crowd out opposing voices. Nuclear weapons issues, however, are important to study in light of a similar concern: the role of technology in public controversies. SDI illustrates how difficult it can be for opposing voices to object to a program grounded in technology in an era which is dominated by technology.

Technology and Public Debate

Nuclear weapons, in a sense, represent humankind's Faustian bargain with technology. The scientific revolution undoubtedly has made life longer, easier, and more enjoyable for many people. But, it has resulted also in the creation of machines that can destroy entire cities in a matter of seconds. Nuclear energy is the ultimate expression of our love-hate relationship with technology.

The intrusion of the technological into almost all the realms of human endeavor has been of interest to scholars in the humanistic tradition.[22] Theorists and critics of discourse have recently entered the fray, focusing on the processes by which the language and logic of technology impact societal discourse. Walter R. Fisher hoped to reclaim "rationality" in discourse for ordinary citizens, thus restoring on a philosophical level the power of human choice and action in a technological world. He wrote:

> I was concerned with the concept of technical reason and the way
> it rendered the public unreasonable; with the idea of rationality

being a matter of argumentative competence in specialized fields, leaving the public and its discourse irrational; with the apparent impossibility of bridging the gaps between experts and the public and between segments of the public; and with the necessity to learn what was supposed to be the essence of persons—rationality—so that one class of citizens can always be superior to another.[23]

Fisher's Narrative Paradigm represented an attempt to redefine the concept of rationality in order to restore power to public, nonexpert voices. Other writers, such as G. Thomas Goodnight, concurred with Fisher's claim that technical discourse overwhelms the public sphere. Goodnight commented on the decline of public deliberative debate in modern society, and the lack of public accountability inherent in technical discourse.[24] Thomas B. Farrell and Goodnight argued, based on an analysis of discourse surrounding the nuclear accident at Three Mile Island, that technical discourse, even as it confronts societal problems, is insulated from social responsibility, and diminishes the power of dissenting voices.[25]

In her study of Reagan's "Star Wars" speech, Janice Hocker Rushing focused on the role of technology in Reagan's vision of strategic defense. She concluded that technology was simultaneously celebrated and constrained in the speech, in that Reagan relied on technology as the solution to the nuclear dilemma, but described its role in the project in mythic terms. She concluded that the mythic form of the speech served to constrain the role of technology in the program.[26] An analysis of pro-SDI discourse contributes to an understanding of the role of technology in public debate. It demonstrates the problems involved in communicating highly technical scientific information to laypersons, and it illustrates how SDI represents a virtual surrendering of the public sphere of discourse to technical rationality.

The alienation and isolation inherent in technologically dominated societies manifests itself in many ways. One of these concerns the lack of citizen control over events and issues that affect the quality of life. Those with expert training and knowledge in any given field, including academic fields, have the power to define and, thereby, control situations affecting individual lives. The citizen becomes a passive recipient of technological expertise, and is granted little or no involvement in the resolution of societal problems. Thus, an ever-widening chasm develops between experts and laypersons, and citizens lose control over their own destinies.

The discourse of the Strategic Defense Initiative program created the illusion of bridging this chasm between scientists and the non-scientific public. Reagan's strong reliance on the American frontier myth in his SDI rhetoric served to make scientists and the lay public consubstantial with one another. The technicians and the citizens were on the same journey; one embodying progress, advancement, and the quest for new knowledge and new frontiers. In other words, in Reagan's SDI rhetoric, the value system of science was transposed upon the American frontier myth in a way that seemed to unify experts and lay citizens for the purpose of accomplishing a shared and noble goal.

This attempt to bridge the gap between experts and citizens was further illustrated in Reagan's use of metaphor. Reagan translated complicated scientific information into metaphors easily understood by persons with no scientific training. In Reagan's terms, SDI was like a roof, or a shield, or an insurance policy, not a complicated system of interlocking and fragile devices that would require years of development before they were ready for testing. Reagan effectively communicated to the public an idea fundamentally grounded in science by translating it into images that related to the everyday experiences of average American citizens.

Upon closer examination, however, this appearance of unity between experts and citizens was merely an illusion, in that Reagan's metaphorical conception of the objectives of the SDI program were not consistent with the objectives espoused by his technical advisers. Reagan's image of a roof that protected a family from rain was not the guiding principle behind the SDI program. Rather, the technical rationality of the defense intellectuals, those who claimed that the uncertainty created by SDI in the minds of Soviet military planners would strengthen deterrence, determined the nature and scope of the program. The version of SDI created for public consumption, a leakproof population defense, shared little or no resemblance with the actual SDI program, a system to protect missile silos from attack. In this sense, the proclaimed unity between the public and the experts in Reagan's rhetorical stance was merely an illusion. Reagan's use of mythic form and metaphor protected the technical realm from challenge, and served to entrench even further the power of technical rationality over social and political questions.

Given this analysis, then, a larger question looms. How is it possible for a speaker to communicate complicated scientific information to the public, while remaining true to both science and society? Is it conceivable that laypersons can be provided with sound technical information on important matters that is neither misleading nor incomplete? Can scientists enter the linguistic realm of the public sphere without the risk of being considered heretics?[27] Who should take the responsibility for communicating scientific information to the public? These questions need to be addressed if citizens are ever to have a say in issues that affect their well-being. Empowerment can only come through understanding, and if vital technical and scientific knowledge is withheld, all members of society lose an opportunity to find solutions to pressing and urgent problems that demand attention.

Although the SDI controversy illustrates the continuing insulation of technology from public challenge, its impact is much more far-reaching, in that SDI *as a concept* represents a complete surrender of the public sphere of deliberation to technology. SDI is merely one example of humankind looking to science and technology to solve pressing social problems. But it is a significant and important example, in that it calls upon technology to solve a problem originally created by technology in the first place. Technological self-perpetuation is evident in the SDI program, not only in the ways in which technicians argued that uncertainty about the program mandated more research, but also in the concept of strategic defense itself. When decision makers embraced SDI and set the program into motion, they surrendered the power of public deliberation to solve the nuclear problem. The best solution to the superpower nuclear arms race and nuclear proliferation, they contended, was a technological fix, not the difficult but vital process of discussion and dialogue that embraces human action, deliberation, decision making, and that which calls for many different voices to share in the public dialogue.

In a post-SDI or post-GPALS world, there would be no need for the United States to make the hard choices involved in negotiating disarmament with the Soviet Union or addressing the underlying causes of nuclear proliferation. The technology of SDI removes the need to do so.

United States officials would not have to worry about trusting Soviet leaders, emerging nuclear nations, or terrorist groups. As Reagan argued, when it came to trusting the Russians or trusting American scientists, he would put his money on American technology anytime. In a world of strategic defense, trusting one's enemies would not be necessary; the machine would take care of that problem.

Embracing a technological solution to the nuclear arms race is symbolically more appealing than embracing a negotiated and deliberative one, precisely because of the nature of technology and the nature of symbol-using beings. It is easier to trust machines than human beings, especially enemies, because machines have no evil motives. Machines exist in the realm of motion, not action, and, as such, make no deliberate choices to deceive or destroy, as enemies are prone to do. Machines are more predictable and consistent than human beings, in that machines are not "rotten with perfection" or "goaded by the spirit of hierarchy."[28] Machines do what humans program them to do, and, if constructed properly, they can perform almost flawlessly.

More importantly, however, a machine like SDI represents the ultimate in the human drive for perfection. The symbol-using creature, having developed a machine capable of obliterating all symbol use itself, has now committed itself to developing a new machine that can transcend and destroy the old machine. Seen in this light, SDI is a *deus ex machina*, but it is one of humanity's own making. Technology, and its human creators, are, therefore, the new gods of this era, representing symbolically a savior to rescue the world from the sin of creating nuclear weapons.

A technological solution to the arms race is godlike in yet another way; it can absolve the U. S. of guilt over past transgressions. SDI provides atonement for past sins. The United States first developed the atomic bomb. The United States is the only nation to have used atomic weapons. The United States first developed the hydrogen bomb. When a nation, so proud of its virtuous and moral heritage and so sure of its destiny to save the world from evil, is confronted with such guilt, either denial of the past or absolute and unfaltering redemption is necessary. A machine like SDI provides redemption for this virtually hidden but everpresent subconscious despair.

Conclusions

Public debate and dialogue—the essence of political communication—are usually considered to be the foundation of democratic society, in that they provide for the exchange of opposing ideas which make citizen governance possible. Given this, the implications of a critical analysis of the symbolic construction of the SDI program are disturbing. In his symbolic construction of SDI, Reagan effectively manipulated the powers of the presidency to name and, therefore, shape and constrain foreign policy debate in this country. His discursive construction of SDI served to insulate the program from effective opposition by identifying SDI with quintessentially American ideals, by using metaphor to communicate complicated scientific information to the public and by providing the illusion of unifying the public with technical experts. In his symbolic construction of the Gulf War and GPALS, Bush transformed the manichean dualism of the East-West conflict into the North-South arena, thereby, perpetuating the ideology of colonialism and reinforcing dualistic structures of meaning that stifle dissent.

Furthermore, technical advisers insulated the program from criticism by importing techniques of scientific rationality into the political sphere. When questioned about future implications of SDI, including cost, potential effectiveness, and the chances for Soviet misperception of the program, they responded as any good scientist would, and claimed that more research would be needed to answer those questions. Thus, the program gained self-perpetuating momentum as uncertainty begat more research, which begat more uncertainty, and so on. Public accountability for the SDI program was diminished when Congressional leaders were forced to make funding decisions under conditions of great uncertainty.

In this way, the SDI debate underscores the way in which two different language communities—the moralistic and the technical—can work together to further ideological goals and constrain public debate over vital national issues. Reagan's stance, the moralistic one, ironically removed public responsibility to act against the nuclear arms race, in that it shielded the other language community—the technical—from criticism. These two language communities overlapped in the SDI controversy, and served mutually-reinforcing purposes.

Reagan's moralistic stance would not have been effective without the support of the technological community; he needed at least some testimony that his version of SDI would be technically feasible. Without this grounding in technical "fact," his vision of a post-SDI world would be dismissed as mere fantasy. Simultaneously, the rhetorical stance of the administration's technical community would not be effective without Reagan's moralistic perspective. The massive investment of time, effort, and money required for the project necessitated an equally massive and compelling rationale for the project, if it was to garner any support at all. What more compelling rationales exist other than making nuclear weapons impotent and obsolete or protecting U. S. territory from nuclear strikes by irrational, maniacal tyrants and terrorists? In this way, two seemingly incommensurate language communities, and their respective worldviews, came together in support of a controversial goal.

The SDI concept itself further infringed upon the sphere of public debate, in that a technological solution to the nuclear arms dilemma removed any need for human choice and action in this area. There is no need for public debate over a nuclear weapons freeze proposal, for example, if a technological gadget can remove the fear and worry of nuclear war from the public's mind. There is no need to develop a longstanding trust of the Soviet Union or an equitable relationship with "Third World" nations, if there is no need to fear their nuclear missiles. There is no need to face the never-ending quest for perfection through technology, if the negative implications of that technology are kept at bay through even more technology.

Future research in this area should consider several issues, some of which are ongoing controversies, and others that deserve closer critical attention. First, what is the role of presidential power in discourse concerning foreign affairs? How is the institutional power of the president incorporated and translated into symbolic power, especially in times of national crisis? Second, what are some alternatives to the dualistic rhetorical forms reproduced in U. S. foreign policy? How, if at all, can critical analyses of foreign policy open up alternative worldviews that are not dependent on oppositional, hierarchical, or priveleged assumptions? Third, how can critical readings of U. S. foreign policy treat the issues surrounding the proliferation of weapons of mass destruction, given its dangerous implications? Fourth, how can postmodern critiques of international relations, in particular, contribute to the ongoing dialogue concerning these issues in other disciplines? My thoughts in these areas do not, of course, represent a final word. I can only hope that others will reflect critically on these issues, engage the dialogue, and participate in an ongoing conversation concerning United States foreign policy discourse.

Notes

Chapter 1.

1. Kenneth Burke, *Permanence and Change* (Berkeley: University of California Press, 1984). See especially chapter 1, "Orientation."

2. The text of Reagan's speech is found in United States, Office of the Federal Register, *Weekly Compilation of Presidential Documents* Washington: GPO, (28 March 1983) 442–448.

3. Robert Scheer, "Scientists Split Over 'Star Wars.'" *Los Angeles Times* 24 September 1985, Part I: 24; see also Steven R. Weisman, "Reagan Says Plan on Missile Defense Will Prevent War," *New York Times* 26 March 1983: 1.

4. See, for example, Stephen J. Cimbala, ed. *The Technology, Strategy and Politics of SDI* (Boulder: Westview Press, 1987); Steven E. Miller and Stephen VanEvera, eds. *The Star Wars Controversy* (Princeton: Princeton University Press, 1986); Bhupendra Jasani, ed. *Space Weapons and International Security* (Oxford: Oxford University Press, 1987); Steven W. Guerrier and Wayne C. Thompson, eds. *Perspectives on Strategic Defense* (Boulder: Westview Press, 1987); Leon Sloss, "The Return of Strategic Defense," *Strategic Review* 12 (Summer 1984): 37–44; Werner Kaltefleiter, "Strategic Defense on the Broader Historical Stage," *Strategic Review* 13 (Summer 1985): 14–21; Marc Geneste, "Strategic Defense and the Shield of Europe," *Strategic Review* 13 (Spring 1985): 37–43; David B. Rivkin, Jr., "SDI: Strategic Reality or Never-Never Land?" *Strategic Review* 15 (Summer 1987): 43–54; James R. Schlesinger, "Rhetoric and Realities in the Star

Wars Debate," *International Security* 10 (Summer 1985): 3–12; Fred S. Hoffman, "The SDI in U. S. Nuclear Strategy," *International Security* 10 (Summer 1985): 13–24; Charles L. Glaser, "Do We Want the Missile Defenses We Can Build?" *International Security* 10 (Summer 1985): 25–57; Francis X. Kane, et al., "Strategic Defenses and Deterrence: A Strategic–Operational Assessment," *Strategic Review* 17 (Winter 1989): 41–54; McGeorge Bundy, et al., "The President's Choice: Star Wars or Arms Control," *Foreign Affairs* 63 (Winter 1984/85): 264–278; Keith B. Payne and Colin S. Gray, "Nuclear Policy and the Defensive Transition," *Foreign Affairs* 62 (1984): 820–842; William E. Burrows, "Ballistic Missile Defense: The Illusion of Security," *Foreign Affairs* 62 (1986): 843–856; Jerome Slater and David Gold Fischer, "Can SDI Provide a Defense?" *Political Science Quarterly* 101 (1986): 839–856.

5. For excellent examples of such post-structuralist critiques, see James DerDerian and Michael J. Shapiro, eds. *International/Intertextual Relations: Postmodern Readings of World Politics* (Lexington, MA: Lexington Books, 1989).

6. Jacques Derrida, "No Apocalypse, Not Now (full speed ahead, seven missiles, seven missives)," *Diacritics* (Summer 1984): 23.

7. See for example, United States, Office of Technology Assessment, *The Effects of Nuclear War* (Washington: GPO, 1979).

8. Derrida 23.

9. Timothy W. Luke, "'What's Wrong With Deterrence?' A Semiotic Interpretation of National Security Policy," in DerDerian and Shapiro 207–229.

10. Kenneth Burke, *Language as Symbolic Action* (Berkeley: University of California Press, 1966) 16.

11. Hugh Dalziel Duncan, introduction to *Permanence and Change*, by Kenneth Burke (Berkeley: University of California Press, 1984) xv.

12. Ira Chernus, *Dr. Strangegod: On the Symbolic Meaning of Nuclear Weapons* (Columbia: University of South Carolina Press, 1986) 8–9.

13. DerDerian and Shapiro's book, a series of essays critiquing international politics and the dominant theoretical approaches in the fields of

international relations, strategic studies, and political science, is an example of the recent trend toward explaining the importance of language, discourse, and text in international politics. See note 5. Additionally, Carol Cohn's essay, "Sex and Death in the Rational World of Defense Intellectuals," *Signs: Journal of Women in Culture and Society* 12 (1987): 687–718, explores these issues from a feminist perspective, with an eye toward the phallocentric tendencies in strategic nuclear discourse and language.

14. Robert L. Ivie, "Images of Savagery in American Justifications for War," *Communication Monographs* 47 (1980): 279–294; Robert L. Ivie, "Speaking 'Common Sense' About the Soviet Threat: Reagan's Rhetorical Stance," *Western Journal of Speech Communication* 48 (1984): 39–50. For similar approaches, see Ronald F. Reid, "New England Rhetoric and the French War, 1754–1760: A Case Study in the Rhetoric of War," *Communication Monographs* 43 (1976): 259–286, and G. Thomas Goodnight, "Ronald Reagan's Re-formulation of the Rhetoric of War: Analysis of the 'Zero Option,' 'Evil Empire,' and 'Star Wars' Addresses," *Quarterly Journal of Speech* 72 (1986): 390–414.

15. See James R. Andrews, "They Chose the Sword: Appeals to War in Nineteenth-Century American Public Address," *Today's Speech* 17 (1969): 3–8; Richard A. Cherwitz, "Lyndon Johnson and the 'Crisis' of Tonkin Gulf: A President's Justification of War," *Western Journal of Speech Communication* 42 (1978): 93–104; F. Michael Smith, "Rhetorical Implications of the 'Aggression' Thesis in the Johnson Administration's Vietnam Argumentation," *Central States Speech Journal* 23 (1972): 217–224; Robert L. Ivie, "The Metaphor of Force in Prowar Discourse: The Case of 1812," *Quarterly Journal of Speech* 68 (1982): 240–253; and Robert L. Ivie, "Presidential Motives for War," *Quarterly Journal of Speech* 60 (1974): 337–345.

16. See Thomas A. Hollihan, "The Public Controversy Over the Panama Canal Treaties: An Analysis of American Foreign Policy Rhetoric," *Western Journal of Speech Communication* 50 (1986): 368–387; J. Michael Hogan, "Public Opinion and American Foreign Policy: The Case of Illusory Support for the Panama Canal Treaties," *Quarterly Journal of Speech* 71 (1985): 302–317; Robert P. Newman, "Lethal Rhetoric: The Selling of the China Myths," *Quarterly Journal of Speech* 61 (1975):

113–128; David E. Procter, "The Rescue Mission: Assigning Guilt to a Chaotic Scene," *Western Journal of Speech Communication* 51 (1987): 245–255.

17. Janice Hocker Rushing, "Ronald Reagan's 'Star Wars' Address: Mythic Containment of Technical Reasoning," *Quarterly Journal of Speech* 72 (1986): 420–423.

18. Philip Wander, "The Rhetoric of American Foreign Policy," *Quarterly Journal of Speech* 70 (1984): 339–361.

19. G. Thomas Goodnight, "The Personal, Technical, and Public Spheres of Argument: A Speculative Inquiry Into the Art of Public Deliberation," *Journal of the American Forensic Association* 18 (1982): 214–227; G. Thomas Goodnight, "On Questions of Evacuation and Survival in Nuclear Conflict: A Case Study in Public Argument and Rhetorical Criticism," *Argument in Transition: Proceedings of the Third Summer Conference on Argumentation,* eds. David Zarefsky, Malcolm Sillars and Jack Rhodes (Annandale, VA: Speech Communication Association, 1983) 319–338.

20. Walter R. Fisher, *Human Communication as Narration: Toward a Philosophy of Reason, Value, and Action* (Columbia: University of South Carolina Press, 1987).

21. Goodnight, "Ronald Reagan's Re-formulation;" Rushing.

22. Rushing 425–426.

23. For an explanation of the connection between Burke's conception of language and the nuclear arms race, see David Cratis Williams, "Nuclear Criticism: In Pursuit of a 'Politically Enabling' Deconstructive Voice," *Journal of the American Forensic Association* 24 (1988): 193–205; and Barry Brummett, "Perfection and the Bomb: Nuclear Weapons, Teleology, and Motives," *Journal of Communication* 39 (Winter 1989): 85–95.

24. Burke, *Language* 16.

25. Burke, *A Rhetoric of Motives* (Berkeley: University of California Press, 1969) 41.

26. Burke, *A Rhetoric* 43.

27. There is controversy concerning whether dramatism is to be

taken as a metaphor or literally. Burke's writings seem to suggest to me that he intends it to be a literal description of human action.

28. Burke, *Permanence and Change* 6–7.

29. Burke, *Permanence and Change* 71.

30. Burke, *Permanence and Change* 173.

31. Burke, *A Grammar of Motives* (Berkeley: University of California Press, 1969) 14; 227–274.

32. Burke, *A Grammar* 12.

33. Burke, *A Grammar* 20; 171–226.

34. Burke, *A Grammar* 275–320.

35. Burke, *A Grammar* xxiv.

36. John Lewis Gaddis, *Strategies of Containment* (New York: Oxford University Press, 1982) 148.

37. Quoted by Gaddis 150.

38. Gaddis 203.

39. Jerome H. Kahan, *Security in the Nuclear Age* (Washington D.C.: The Brookings Institution, 1975) 92–93.

40. Kahan 94–96.

41. This is not to say, however, that no changes in nuclear policy have occurred since 1963. However, Gaddis argues that the Nixon Doctrine, which was continued by Ford, represented in many ways a return to asymmetrical response (304). Kahan argues that Carter's emphasis on counterforce targeting in many ways still relied upon mutually assured destruction at its core (225). My point is simply that MAD is still with us, if not at the intricate level of strategic targeting, then at the level of public policy justification.

42. Fred Halliday, *The Making of the Second Cold War* (London: Verso Editions, 1986) 73.

43. Halliday 235.

44. Halliday 235.

45. Michael Mandelbaum and Strobe Talbott, *Reagan and Gorbachev* (New York: Vintage Books, 1987) 43. For an excellent rhetorical analysis

of this speech and others by Reagan, see G. Thomas Goodnight, "Ronald Reagan's Reformulation of the Rhetoric of War: Analysis of the 'Zero Option,' 'Evil Empire,' and 'Star Wars' Addresses." *Quarterly Journal of Speech* 72 (1986): 390–414.

46. Quoted in Paul M. Cole, "The Reagan Administration's Reaction to the Nuclear Weapons Freeze Movement," *The Nuclear Freeze Debate: Arms Control Issues for the 1980s*, eds. Paul M. Cole and William J. Taylor (Boulder, CO: Westview Press, 1983) 97.

47. For an outstanding discussion of the relationship between nuclear weapons and traditional religious symbols, see Ira Chernus, *Dr. Strangegod: On the Symbolic Meaning of Nuclear Weapons* (Columbia: University of South Carolina Press, 1986).

48. Jonathan Schell, *The Fate of the Earth* (New York: Alfred A. Knopf, 1982) 194.

49. Paul Boyer, "From Activism to Apathy: The American People and Nuclear Weapons, 1963–1980," *The Journal of American History* 70 (1984): 821–844.

50. Adam M. Garfinkle, *The Politics of the Nuclear Freeze* (Philadelphia: Foreign Policy Research Institute, 1984) 6.

51. Garfinkle 80.

52. Editorial, *The Houston Post* 17 March 1982, *Editorials on File* 13 (March 16–31, 1982): 307.

53. *Editorials on File* 13 (March 16–31, 1982): 306.

54. Garfinkle 90.

55. *Editorials on File* 13 (June 1–15, 1982): 646.

56. Quoted in *Editorials on File* 13 (August 1–15, 1982): 875. Garfinkle (90) points out that the freeze resolution eventually passed the Congress, in watered-down form, in May, 1983.

57. Edward F. Feighan, "The Freeze in Congress," Cole and Taylor 29.

58. Quoted in Robert Scheer, "'Star Wars': A Program in Dissarray," *Los Angeles Times* 22 September 1985: 14.

59. *Weekly Compilation of Presidential Documents* 28 March 1983: 447.

60. *Weekly Compilation of Presidential Documents* 28 March 1983: 447.

61. *Weekly Compilation of Presidential Documents* 28 March 1983: 448.

62. For an excellent analysis of Reagan's rhetorical use of the theme of time in this speech, see Janice Hocker Rushing, "Ronald Reagan's 'Star Wars' Address: Mythic Containment of Technical Reasoning," *Quarterly Journal of Speech* 72 (1986): 415–433.

Chapter 2.

1. E. Culpepper Clark, "Argument and Historical Analysis," *Advances in Argumentation Theory and Research*, eds. J. Robert Cox and Charles Arthur Willard (Carbondale, IL: Southern Illinois University Press, 1982) 298–317.

2. Richard K. Ashley, "Living on Border Lines: Man, Poststructuralism, and War," in James DerDerian and Michael J. Shapiro, eds. *International/Intertextual Relations: Postmodern Readings of World Politics* (Lexington, MA: Lexington Books, 1989): 259–321.

3. Hans J. Morgenthau, *The Purpose of American Politics* (New York: Alfred A. Knopf, 1960) 13.

4. Lloyd C. Gardner, Walter F. LaFeber, and Thomas J. McCormick, *Creation of the American Empire* (Chicago: Rand McNally, 1973) 4.

5. Ernest Bormann traces the development of rhetorical constructions of the American Dream, from Puritan religious rhetoric through the time of Abraham Lincoln. See Ernest G. Bormann, *The Force of Fantasy: Restoring the American Dream* (Carbondale, IL: Southern Illinois University Press, 1985).

6. James Oliver Robertson, *American Myths, American Reality* (New York: Hill & Wang, 1980) 31.

7. Reinhold Niebuhr, *The Irony of American History* (New York: Charles Scribner's Sons, 1952) 24.

8. Ralph B. Potter, *War and Moral Discourse* (Richmond, VA: John Knox Press, 1969) 58.

9. Morgenthau 7–8.

10. Morgenthau 11. For an interesting explanation of the role of these ideas in American foreign policy, see Samuel P. Huntington, "American Ideals versus American Institutions," *Political Science Quarterly* 97 (1982): 1–37.

11. Paul Merrill Spurlin, *The French Enlightenment in America* (Athens: University of Georgia Press, 1984) 77.

12. Spurlin 77.

13. Spurlin 7.

14. Gerald Stourzh, *Benjamin Franklin and American Foreign Policy* (Chicago: University of Chicago Press, 1969) 22.

15. Niebuhr 25.

16. Gardner, et al 64.

17. John Spanier, *American Foreign Policy Since World War II* Ninth Edition (New York: Holt, Rinehart and Winston, 1983) 5.

18. Stourzh 5.

19. Stourzh 2.

20. See Stourzh for a complete discussion of Franklin's political philosophy and his views on American foreign policy.

21. Quoted in Spurlin 10.

22. For a discussion of the concept of "social knowledge," see Thomas B. Farrell, "Knowledge, Consensus, and Rhetorical Theory," *Quarterly Journal of Speech* 62 (1976): 1–14; and Farrell, "Social Knowledge II," *Quarterly Journal of Speech* 64 (1978): 329–334.

23. George Washington, "Farewell Address," *Select Orations Illustrating American Political History*, ed. Samuel Bannister Harding (New York: Macmillan, 1919) 162.

24. Gardner, et al 20.

25. Gardner, et al 20.

26. Gardner, et al 42.

27. Gardner, et al 63–64.

28. Gardner, et al 12.

29. Gardner, et al 111. For a full account of the Monroe Doctrine, see Ernest R. May, *The Making of the Monroe Doctrine* (Cambridge: Harvard University Press, 1975).

30. Gardner, et al 111–112.

31. For an extended discussion of these factors, see Gardner, et al.

32. As quoted in Gardner, et al 224.

33. Gardner, et al 221–225.

34. Arthur S. Link, *American Epoch: A History of the United States Since the 1890s*, 3 vols. (New York: Alfred A. Knopf, 1967) 1: 3.

35. Robertson 73–74.

36. Gardner, et al (pp. 255–256) argued that McKinley's "Open Door" policy with China required a stable and continuing U. S. military presence in the Philippines.

37. Claude G. Bowers, *Beveridge and the Progressive Era* (New York: The Literary Guild, 1932).

38. For an analysis of Beveridge's imperialist and progressive rhetoric, see A. Cheree Carlson, "Albert J. Beveridge as Imperialist and Progressive: The Means Justify the Ends," *Western Journal of Speech Communication* 52 (1988): 46–62.

39. Link, *American Epoch* 16.

40. Link, *American Epoch* 155–161.

41. Woodrow Wilson, quoted in Perry E. Giankos and Albert Karson, eds., *American Diplomacy and the Sense of Destiny*, 4 vols. (Belmont, CA: Wadsworth Publishing Co., 1966) 2: 58.

42. Norman A. Graebner, *America as a World Power: A Realist Appraisal from Wilson to Reagan* (Wilmington: Scholarly Resources Incorporated, 1984) xvii–xviii.

43. Ronald Steel, *Walter Lippman and the American Century* (New York: Vintage Books, 1980) 94.

44. Link, *American Epoch* 173.

45. Steel 93–95; Arthur S. Link, *The Impact of World War I* (New York: Harper and Row, 1969) 11–15.

46. Arthur S. Link, *Wilson*, 5 vols. (Princeton: Princeton University Press, 1965) 5: 5.

47. Link, *Wilson* 35–36.

48. Link, *Wilson* 106–108.

49. Link, *Wilson* 162.

50. Link, *Wilson* 149.

51. Graebner xxvi–xxvii.

52. Steel 89.

53. Link, *Wilson* 396–397.

54. Link, *Wilson* 415–417.

55. Wilson 62.

56. Wilson 64.

57. Barbara W. Tuchman, *The Guns of August* (New York: MacMillan, 1962) 336–337; Graebner, in chapter 1, surveys the various points of view on the issue of U. S. moral leadership during World War I and immediately thereafter.

58. Morgenthau 107.

59. Ralph A. Stone, introduction to *Wilson and the League of Nations*, ed. Ralph A. Stone (New York: Holt, Rinehart and Winston, 1967) 1.

60. W. Stull Holt, "Playing Politics With the League," Stone 28–29.

61. Graebner, chapter 1.

62. Selig Adler, "The Isolationist Impulse," Stone 41.

63. Adler 41–42.

64. As quoted in Graebner 37.

65. McCormick 19.

66. Graebner 86.

67. Russell F. Weigley, *The American Way of War* (New York: Macmillan, 1973); James W. Hikins, "The Rhetoric of 'Unconditional Surrender' and the Decision to Drop the Atomic Bomb," *Quarterly Journal of Speech* 69 (1983): 379–400.

68. John Lewis Gaddis, *The United States and the Origins of the Cold War 1941–1947.* (New York: Columbia University Press, 1972) 1–8.

69. Potter 59.

70. See Hikins.

71. Paul Boyer, *By the Bomb's Early Light (New York: Pantheon Books, 1985).* See especially chapter 3.

72. For a thorough discussion of the controversy over containment, see John Lewis Gaddis, *Strategies of Containment* (New York: Oxford University Press, 1982), especially chapters 2–4. See also *Containment: Documents on American Policy and Strategy, 1945–1950,* eds. Thomas H. Etzold and John Lewis Gaddis (New York: Columbia University Press, 1978).

73. Wayne Brockriede and Robert L. Scott, *Moments in the Rhetoric of the Cold War* (New York: Random House, 1970); Philip Wander, "The Rhetoric of American Foreign Policy," *Quarterly Journal of Speech* 70 (1984): 339–361.

74. As quoted in Graebner 173.

75. Graebner 212.

76. Robertson 339.

77. Robert W. Tucker, *A New Isolationism: Threat or Promise?* (New York: Universe Books, 1972).

78. McCormick 88.

79. McCormick 97–98.

80. For examples of Reagan's Cold War rhetoric, see G. Thomas Goodnight, "Ronald Reagan's Re-formulation of the Rhetoric of War: Analysis of the 'Zero Option,' 'Evil Empire,' and 'Star Wars' Addresses," *Quarterly Journal of Speech* 72 (1986): 400–403.

81. George Bush, "Toward a New World Order," *U. S. Department of State Dispatch* 17 September 1990: 91.

82. Niebuhr 2.

83. Morgenthau 177.

Chapter 3

1. Jan H. Kalicki, "Arms Control and the Nuclear Weapons Freeze," *The Nuclear Weapons Freeze and Arms Control,* Proceedings of a Sympo-

sium held at the American Academy of Arts and Sciences, January 13–15, 1983 (Cambridge: President and Fellows of Harvard College, 1983) 13.

2. Quoted in Robert Scheer, "'Star Wars': A Program in Disarray," *The Los Angeles Times* 22 September 1985: 14.

3. Paul Boyer, *By the Bomb's Early Light* (New York: Pantheon Books, 1985) 183.

4. Boyer 188–189; Robert L. Spaeth, *No Easy Answers: Christians Debate Nuclear Arms* (Minneapolis: Winston Press, 1983) 12.

5. Boyer 185–187.

6. Louis N. Ridenour, "Science and Secrecy," *The American Scholar* 15 (April 1946): 151.

7. Nathaniel Peffer, "Politics is Peace," *The American Scholar* 15 (April 1946): 160.

8. Boyer 282.

9. Quoted in Boyer 197.

10. Quoted in Boyer 200.

11. Boyer 202.

12. Boyer 229.

13. See David Henry, "Idealism vs. Realism: Campaign Rhetoric in the Scientists' Movement, 1945–1962," paper presented at the Annual Meeting of the Western Speech Communication Association, San Diego, CA, February 1988; see also Boyer, especially chapter 3.

14. Boyer 352–355.

15. Charles-Philippe David, *Debating Counterforce* (Boulder: Westview Press, 1987).

16. David 168–172. Jerome H. Kahan, *Security in the Nuclear Age* (Washington, DC: Brookings Institution, 1975) traces this philosophy back to Robert McNamara's "No Cities" doctrine during the Kennedy Administration. For an alternative view, see Stephen J. Cimbala, *Rethinking Nuclear Strategy* (Wilmington: Scholarly Resources, Inc., 1988). Cimbala argues that, although declaratory policy has embraced counterforce, actual technical capabilities tend toward an operative strategy of mutual retaliation.

17. Alexander Cockburn and James Ridgeway, "The Freeze Movement Versus Reagan," *New Left Review* 137 (1983): 7–10.

18. Quoted in David 179.

19. For a discussion of these proposed civil defense relocation plans, see Robert Scheer, *With Enough Shovels: Reagan, Bush and Nuclear War* (New York: Random House, 1982).

20. For a sample of this debate, see Walter R. Fisher and Richard Dean Burns, eds. *Armament and Disarmament: The Continuing Dispute* (Belmont, CA: Wadsworth, 1964): 58–76.

21. Elizabeth Walker Mechling and Jay Mechling, "The Campaign for Civil Defense and the Struggle to Naturalize the Bomb," *Western Journal of Speech Communication* 55 (1991): 105–133.

22. Robert F. Drinan, *Beyond the Nuclear Freeze* (New York: The Seabury Press, 1983) 2–3.

23. Edward M. Kennedy and Mark O. Hatfield, *Freeze! How You Can Help Prevent Nuclear War* (New York: Bantam Books, 1982) 97.

24. Michael Mandelbaum and Strobe Talbott, *Reagan and Gorbachev* (New York: Vintage Books, 1987) 27–30.

25. Louis Harris, "Public Opinion and the Freeze Movement," *The Nuclear Weapons Freeze and Arms Control* 39.

26. Harry C. Boyte, "The Foundation of the New Peace Movement: A Communitarian Perspective," *Social Policy* 13 (1982): 6.

27. Adam M. Garfinkle, *The Politics of the Nuclear Freeze* (Philadelphia: Foreign Policy Research Institute, 1984) 80.

28. Douglas C. Waller, "The Impact of the Nuclear Freeze Movement on Congress," *The Nuclear Weapons Freeze and Arms Control* 48.

29. Harris 39–40.

30. *Editorials on File* 13 (June 1–15, 1982): 646.

31. Leland Griffin, "A Dramatistic Theory of the Rhetoric of Movements," William Rueckert, ed., *Critical Responses to Kenneth Burke* (Minneapolis: University of Minnesota Press, 1969) 456–478. A dramatistic perspective on social movements is, of course, one of many theoretical perspectives available to a critic of movement discourse. Sociological

approaches, historical approaches, psychological approaches, and post-structuralist approaches are also present in this voluminous literature. For examples of these other approaches, see Robert A. Goldberg, *Grassroots Resistance: Social Movements in Twentieth Century America* (Belmont, CA: Wadsworth, 1991); Charles Stewart, Craig Smith, and Robert E. Denton, *Persuasion and Social Movements* (Prospect Heights, IL: Waveland Press, 1984); Herbert W. Simons, Elizabeth W. Mechling, and Howard N. Schrier, "The Functions of Human Communication in Mobilizing for Action from the Bottom Up: The Rhetoric of Social Movements," in Carroll C. Arnold and John Waite Bowers, eds., *Handbook on Rhetorical and Communication Theory* (Boston: Allyn & Bacon, 1984–1985): 792–867; Michael Calvin McGee, "'Social Movement': Phenomenon or Meaning?" *Central States Speech Journal* 31 (1980): 233–244. I chose a dramatistic perspective here for the reasons I outline in chapter 1.

32. Griffin 460.

33. James L. Hart, "The Case for a Freeze on Nuclear Arms," *America* 23 October 1982: 226.

34. Drinan 75.

35. Bernard T. Feld, "A Mutual Freeze," *Bulletin of the Atomic Scientists* 38 (May 1982): 3.

36. Jack Mendelsohn, "The Freeze Movement as an Ethical Achievement," *The Nuclear Weapons Freeze and Arms Control* 101.

37. Quoted in Kennedy and Hatfield 25.

38. Drinan 5; Mary Ellen Leary, "Nuclear Freeze: Bishops and Nobel Laureates," *Commonweal* 29 January 1982: 41.

39. Mark O. Hatfield, "Should the U. S. Now Negotiate an 'In-Place' Freeze on Nuclear Weapons?" *Congressional Digest* 61 (August–September 1982): 210.

40. Mendelsohn 100.

41. Kennedy and Hatfield xviii.

42. For an example of Caldicott's rhetoric, see Helen Caldicott, *Missile Envy: The Arms Race and Nuclear War* (New York: Bantam Books, 1985).

43. Caldicott, "A Commitment to Life," *The Humanist* September–October 1982: 9.

44. Caldicott, "A Commitment" 10.

45. Jonathan Schell, *The Fate of the Earth* (New York: Alfred A. Knopf, 1982) 1–96.

46. Kennedy and Hatfield 13.

47. Drinan 22–23.

48. J. Michael Hogan, "Apocalyptic Pornography and the Nuclear Freeze: A Defense of the Public," *Argument and Critical Practices*, ed. Joseph W. Wenzel (Annandale, VA: Speech Communication Association, 1987): 541–548.

49. See Fisher and Burns 85–108, for excerpts from this controversy.

50. Drinan 25.

51. Kennedy and Hatfield 13.

52. Caldicott, "A Commitment" 8–9.

53. Mendelsohn 101.

54. Hatfield 212–214.

55. Kennedy and Hatfield 136.

56. Hart 228.

57. Kennedy and Hatfield 136.

58. Quoted in Kennedy and Hatfield 127.

59. Hatfield 214.

60. Kalicki 14–16.

61. Christopher E. Paine, "Conceptual Foundations of a Comprehensive Nuclear Freeze," *The Nuclear Weapons Freeze and Arms Control* 26–27.

62. Edward M Kennedy, "Nuclear Weapons Freeze Proposal Followed by Major Reductions in the Nuclear Arsenals," *Bulletin of Peace Proposals* 13 (1982): 250.

63. Kennedy and Hatfield 143.

64. Spaeth 1–2.

65. Quoted in Donald L. Davidson, *Nuclear Weapons and the American Churches: Ethical Positions on Modern Warfare* (Boulder: Westview Press, 1983) 187.

66. Davidson 69.

67. Davidson 124–176.

68. National Council of Catholic Bishops, "The Challenge of Peace: God's Promise and Our Response," *Catholics and Nuclear War*, ed. Philip J. Murnion (New York: Crossroad Publishing Co., 1983) 288. For a discussion of the formulation and rhetorical implications of the Pastoral Letter, see Stave Goldzwig and George Cheney, "The U. S. Catholic Bishops on Nuclear Arms: Corporate Advocacy, Role Redefinition, and Rhetorical Adaptation," *Central States Speech Journal* 35 (1984): 8–23.

69. National Council of Catholic Bishops 292.

70. National Council of Catholic Bishops 291.

71. National Council of Catholic Bishops 300–301.

72. Spaeth 25.

73. David Hollenbach, *Nuclear Ethics: A Christian Moral Argument* (New York: Paulist Press, 1983) 73–74.

74. Richard A. McCormick, "Nuclear Deterrence and the Problem of Intention: A Review of the Positions," in Murnion 173.

75. National Council of Catholic Bishops 302.

76. *Editorials on File* 13 (March 16–31, 1982): 306.

77. Harris 39.

78. Kennedy 251.

79. For example, see National Council of Catholic Bishops 318.

80. Christopher M. Lehman, "Arms Control vs. the Freeze," *The Nuclear Weapons Freeze and Arms Control* 67.

81. Jake Garn, "Should the U. S. Now Negotiate an 'In-Place' Freeze on Nuclear Weapons?" *Congressional Digest* 61 (August–September 1982): 215.

82. National Council of Catholic Bishops 326.

Chapter 4.

1. United States, Office of the Federal Register, *Weekly Compilation of Presidential Documents* (Washington: GPO, 28 March 1983) 447.

2. Sources consulted were: *Weekly Compilation of Presidential Documents, Department of State Bulletin,* various Congressional hearings, and other government publications.

3. Kenneth Burke, *A Grammar of Motives* (Berkeley: University of California Press, 1969) 128–170.

4. *Weekly Compilation* 28 March 1983: 447.

5. *Weekly Compilation* 28 March 1983: 443.

6. *Weekly Compilation* 28 March 1983: 447.

7. Burke 287.

8. *Weekly Compilation* 28 March 1983: 447.

9. *Weekly Compilation* 28 March 1983: 448.

10. *Weekly Compilation* 28 March 1983: 448.

11. *Weekly Compilation* 28 March 1983: 448.

12. *Weekly Compilation* 28 March 1983: 448.

13. *Weekly Compilation* 28 March 1983: 447.

14. *Weekly Compilation* 28 March 1983: 448.

15. United States, Congress, Senate, Committee on Foreign Relations, *Strategic Defense and Anti-Satellite Weapons,* 98th Cong., 2nd sess. (Washington: GPO, 1984) 30.

16. Department of Defense, "Defense Against Ballistic Missiles: An Assessment of Technologies and Policy Implications," reprinted in *Strategic Defense and Anti-Satellite Weapons* 124.

17. *Strategic Defense and Anti-Satellite Weapons* 10.

18. *Weekly Compilation* 9 June 1986: 739.

19. Kenneth A. Adelman, "Making Arms Control Work," *Department of State Bulletin* 86 (January 1986): 41.

20. Quoted in Ashton B. Carter, "Directed Energy Missile Defense in Space: Background Paper," reprinted in *Strategic Defense and Anti-Satellite Weapons* 312.

21. *Weekly Compilation* 11 March 1985: 246; 26 August 1985: 996–997.

22. United States, Congress, House, Committee on Armed Services,

Strategic Defense Initiative (SDI) Program, 99th Cong., 1st sess. (Washington: GPO, 1985) 43.

23. *Weekly Compilation* 17 March 1986: 341; 9 June 1986: 739.

24. *Weekly Compilation* 21 July 1986: 940.

25. *Weekly Compilation* 10 November 1986: 1515, 1512; 27 October 1986: 1431.

26. Burke 275–287.

27. *Weekly Compilation* 14 January 1985: 34; 21 January 1985: 58–59; 18 March 1985: 276; 25 March 1985: 322.

28. *Weekly Compilation* 11 November 1985: 1343.

29. *Weekly Compilation* 9 December 1985: 1451–1452.

30. This understanding was apparent even in Reagan's first speech on SDI. *Weekly Compilation* 28 March 1983: 448.

31. *Weekly Compilation* 4 February 1985: 155; 18 February 1985: 172; 11 November 1985: 1359; 25 November 1985: 1427.

32. *Weekly Compilation* 28 March 1983: 447–448.

33. *Weekly Compilation* 23 June 1986: 839.

34. *Weekly Compilation* 28 March 1983: 453.

35. Fred S. Hoffman, "Ballistic Missile Defenses and U. S. National Security," reprinted in *Strategic Defense and Anti-Satellite Weapons* 129.

36. *Strategic Defense and Anti-Satellite Weapons* 25.

37. For a discussion of Reagan's rhetorical stance toward the Soviets, see G. Thomas Goodnight, "Ronald Reagan's Reformulation of the Rhetoric of War: Analysis of the 'Zero Option,' 'Evil Empire,' and 'Star Wars' Addresses," *Quarterly Journal of Speech* 72 (1986): 390–414.

38. *Weekly Compilation* 7 January 1985: 8–9; Paul H. Nitze, "SDI: The Soviet Program," *Department of State Bulletin* 85 (September 1985): 40–42.

39. *Weekly Compilation* 6 May 1985: 556.

40. *Weekly Compilation* 21 October 1985: 1247.

41. *Weekly Compilation* 18 March 1985: 280; 4 November 1985: 1419.

42. *Weekly Compilation* 14 January 1985: 31; 18 April 1985: 395; 23 September 1985: 1101.

43. *Weekly Compilation* 4 November 1985: 1319; 9 December 1985: 1458.

44. *Weekly Compilation* 7 October 1985: 1157; 23 September 1985: 1104.

45. *Weekly Compilation* 11 November 1985: 1346.

46. *Weekly Compilation* 20 October 1986: 1375–1379.

47. Quoted in R. Jeffrey Smith, "Weapons Bureaucracy Spurns Star Wars Goal," reprinted in *Strategic Defense and Anti-Satellite Weapons* 53.

48. *Strategic Defense and Anti-Satellite Weapons* 13, 101; Department of Defense, "Strategic Defense Initiative," *Department of State Bulletin* 84 (May 1984): 71.

49. *Weekly Compilation* 4 February 1985: 154.

50. *Weekly Compilation* 4 February 1985: 154–155.

51. *Weekly Compilation* 18 February 1985: 175.

52. *Weekly Compilation* 1 April 1985: 380.

53. Smith 53.

54. *Weekly Compilation* 16 June 1986: 800; Paul H. Nitze, "SDI, Arms Control, and Stability: Toward a New Synthesis," *Department of State Bulletin* 86 (August 1986): 44; George Schultz, "Reykjavik: A Watershed in U. S.–Soviet Relations," *Department of State Bulletin* 86 (December 1986): 25.

55. Burke, "Definition of Man," *Language as Symbolic Action* (Berkeley: University of California Press, 1966) 4.

56. Burke, "Definition" 13–15.

57. For a thorough explication of this argument, see Randall A. Lake, "Order and Disorder in Anti-Abortion Rhetoric: A Logological View," *Quarterly Journal of Speech* 70 (1984): 425–443. See especially pages 427–428.

58. Burke, "Dramatism," *Drama in Life: The Uses of Communication in Society* Eds. James E. Combs and Michael W. Masfield (New York: Hastings House Publishers, 1976) 10–11.

59. For a discussion of these types of arguments against SDI, see Philip M. Boffey et al., *Claiming the Heavens* (New York: Times Books, 1989) 223–239.

60. Richard N. Perle, *Strategic Defense and Anti-Satellite Weapons* 90; *Weekly Compilation* 3 December 1984: 1843; 14 January 1985: 31; 18 March 1985: 278; 8 April 1985: 395.

61. Paul H. Nitze and Abraham D. Sofaer, "The ABM Treaty and the SDI Program," *Department of State Bulletin* 85 (December 1985): 37–40.

62. *Weekly Compilation* 23 March 1987: 277.

63. *Weekly Compilation* 23 November 1987: 1333; 30 November 1987: 1375; "President Reagan's Address to the Nation, December 10, 1987," *Department of State Bulletin* 88 (February 1988): 20; "Secretary's Interview on 'Face the Nation,'" *Department of State Bulletin* 88 (January 1988): 9.

64. United States, Congress, Senate, Committee on Appropriations, *Department of Defense Authorization for Appropriations for Fiscal Years 1988 and 1989*, 100th Cong., 1st sess. (Washington: GPO, 1987) 2155–2157.

65. *Department of Defense Authorization for Appropriations for Fiscal Years 1988 and 1989. 2188.*

66. Strategic Defense and Anti-Satellite Weapons 69.

67. *Strategic Defense and Anti-Satellite Weapons* 73.

68. *Strategic Defense and Anti-Satellite Weapons* 74.

69. *Strategic Defense and Anti-Satellite Weapons* 72.

70. United States, Congress, Senate, Committee on Appropriations, *Department of Defense Authorization for Appropriations for Fiscal Year 1986*, 99th Cong., 1st sess. (Washington: GPO, 1985) 3636.

71. *Department of Defense Authorization for Appropriations for Fiscal Years 1988 and 1989. 2155, 2188.*

72. For more indepth discussions of this controversy, see Deborah Blum, "Weird Science: Livermore's X-Ray Laser Flap," Bulletin of the Atomic Scientists (July/August 1988): 7–13; Robert Scheer, "The Man Who Blew the Whistle on 'Star Wars,'" *Los Angeles Times Magazine* 17 July 1988: 6+.

73. Dan Morain, "Energy Secretary Warns Weapons Scientists Not to Disagree in Public," *Los Angeles Times* 23 July 1988, Part I: 24.

74. Department of Defense, "Strategic Defense Initiative" 71.

75. *The President's Strategic Defense Initiative* (Washington: The President, 1985) 7.

Chapter 5.

1. Fred Barnes, "Pebbles Go Bam-Bam," *The New Republic* 17 April 1989: 12–13.

2. Andrew Rosenthal, "Tower Declares 'Star Wars' Shield Can't be Complete," *New York Times* 27 January 1989: A12.

3. Richard Halloran, "As Pentagon Budget Unfolds, Space Missile Shield is Intact," *New York Times* 2 March 1989: B11.

4. As quoted in Rosenthal A1.

5. Rosenthal A12.

6. "Bush May Keep Midgetman Despite Cheney," *Salt Lake Tribune* 22 April 1989: A2.

7. Richard Burt, "Nuclear and Space Talks Open Round Eleven," *Department of State Bulletin* (August 1989): 74.

8. Henry F. Cooper, "Status of the Defense and Space Talks," *Department of State Bulletin* (October 1989): 20.

9. George Bush, "Security Strategy for the 1990s," *Department of State Bulletin* (July 1989): 20.

10. See William M. Arkin, "Gorbachev Talks But Who Listens?" *Bulletin of the Atomic Scientists* (January–February 1989): 17.

11. "Secretary's Interview on 'Face the Nation,' September 24, 1989," *Department of State Bulletin* (November 1989): 15.

12. Arkin 5.

13. Hans A. Bethe, "Chop Down the Nuclear Arsenals," *Bulletin of the Atomic Scientists* (March 1989): 12.

14. James Baker, "The International Agenda and the Fiscal Year 1990 Budget Request," *Department of State Bulletin* (April 1989): 18.

15. George Bush, "Change in the Soviet Union," *Department of State Bulletin* (July 1989): 16.

16. James Baker, "From Points to Pathways of Mutual Advantage:

Next Steps in Soviet–American Relations," *U. S. Department of State Dispatch* 22 October 1990: 199.

17. Quoted in Marcia Dunn, "New SDI: Icing on Stale Cake or Savior for U. S. Defense?" *Salt Lake Tribune* 31 March 1991: A8.

18. Barnes 13; "Too Brilliant by Half," *The New Republic* 29 May 1989: 7; Gary Chapman, "Smart Rocks, Brilliant Pebbles, Genius Dust?" *Bulletin of the Atomic Scientists* (November 1989): 11.

19. Donna Cassata, "Senate OK's $289 Billion Defense Bill," *Salt Lake Tribune* 5 August 1990: A1. This concern over brilliant pebbles continued, as illustrated by the House of Representatives' vote to eliminate funding for the program on May 22, 1991. Eric Schmitt, "House Approves Military Budget, Cutting B–2 and 'Star Wars' Funds," *New York Times* 23 May 1991: A1–C18.

20. United States, Congress, House, Subcommittee on Legislation and National Security of the Committee on Government Operations, *Cost Estimates for Phase I of the Strategic Defense Initiative*, 101st Cong., 1st sess. (Washington, DC: GPO, 1989) 48.

21. *Cost Estimates for Phase I of the Strategic Defense Initiative* 34.

22. "Conference Fallout," *Bulletin of the Atomic Scientists* (December 1990): 4.

23. Colin Norman, "SDI Heads for Fiscal Crash," *Science* 247 (16 March 1990): 1285.

24. George Bush, "The Arabian Peninsula: U. S. Principles," *U. S. Department of State Dispatch* 3 September 1990: 53.

25. James Baker, "America's Stake in the Persian Gulf," *U. S. Department of State Dispatch* 10 September 1990: 69.

26. Baker, "America's Stake" 69.

27. George Bush, "The UN: World Parliament of Peace," *U. S. Department of State Dispatch* 8 October 1990: 151.

28. Bush, "The Arabian Peninsula" 53.

29. Dan Quayle, "America's Objectives in the Persian Gulf," *U. S. Department of State Dispatch* 10 December 1990: 312.

30. Bush, "America's Stand Against Aggression," *U. S. Department of State Dispatch* 3 September 1990: 55.

31. Bush, "The Arabian Peninsula" 53.

32. Bush, "The Arabian Peninsula" 52; Bush, "Against Aggression in the Persian Gulf," *U. S. Department of State Dispatch* 3 September 1990: 54.

33. Baker, "America's Stake" 69; Bush, "Against Aggression" 54; Bush, "Toward a New World Order," *U. S. Department of State Dispatch* 17 September 1990: 92.

34. Baker, "America's Stake" 69; Bush, "Toward a New World Order" 91; Bush, "Thanksgiving Day Address to U. S. Forces in Saudi Arabia," *U. S. Department of State Dispatch* 26 November 1990: 279.

35. Bush, "Thanksgiving Day" 279.

36. Bush, "America's Stand" 55.

37. Bush, "Remarks to U. S. Troops," *U. S. Department of State Dispatch* 12 November 1990: 260.

38. Bush, "The Arabian Peninsula" 52; Bush, "America's Stand" 55; Bush, "The UN" 151.

39. Baker, "America's Stake" 70.

40. Bush, "The Arabian Peninsula" 52.

41. Quayle, "America's Objectives" 310.

42. Baker, "Why America is in the Gulf," *U. S. Department of State Dispatch* 5 November 1990: 235.

43. Baker, "America's Stake" 71.

44. Bush, "The UN" 152.

45. Bush, "The UN" 152.

46. Bush, "The UN" 153.

47. Bush, "The UN" 153.

48. James Baker, "Recent Developments in US–Soviet Relations," *U. S. Department of State Dispatch* 3 September 1990: 46.

49. James Baker, "U. S. Foreign Policy Priorities and Fiscal Year 1991 Budget," *U. S. Department of State Dispatch* 3 September 1990: 1.

50. Baker, "From Points to Pathways" 201.

51. Dunn A8; "After the Patriot," *Wall Street Journal* 23 January 1991: A12.

52. John Pike, "Qaddafi Goes Ballistic," *The New Republic* 20 March 1989: 14–16.

53. Michael Krepon, "Don't Parrot Old Arguments on Missile Defense," *Bulletin of the Atomic Scientists* (January–February 1991): 13.

54. Quoted in Mark Thompson, "Command System, High-Tech Weapons Win High Marks," *Salt Lake Tribune* 10 March 1991: 4A.

55. Ken Adelman, "Star Wars in the Desert," *Newsweek* 4 February 1991: 14.

56. "After the Patriot" A12.

57. Keith B. Payne, *Missile Defense in the 21st Century: Protection Against Limited Threats* (Boulder: Westview Press, 1991) 28–29.

58. George Bush, "State of the Union Address," *U. S. Department of State Dispatch* 4 February 1991: 66.

59. Edward W. Said, "Representing the Colonized: Anthropology's Interlocutors," *Critical Inquiry* 15 (Winter 1989): 205–225.

60. Said, "Representing" 206.

61. Said, "Representing" 207.

62. Said, "Representing" 207.

63. Abdul R. Jan Mohamed, "The Economy of Manichean Allegory: The Function of Racial Difference in Colonialist Literature," *Critical Inquiry* 12 (Autumn 1985): 64.

64. Said, "Representing" 209–210.

65. Edward W. Said, *Orientalism* (New York: Vintage Books, 1979).

66. Cheney, quoted in Payne 61–62.

67. Payne 46–47.

68. Baker, "Remarks to U. S. Troops," *U. S. Department of State Dispatch* 12 November 1990: 260; Bush, "State of the Union Address" 67.

69. Payne 32.

70. Jan Mohamed 63.

71. Payne 97.

72. Pike 15.

73. Payne 50.

74. Payne 54.

75. Payne 48.

Chapter 6.

1. W. Lance Bennett, *Public Opinion in American Politics* (New York: Harcourt Brace Jovanovich, 1980) 30–33.

2. James A. Nathan and James K. Oliver, *Foreign Policy Making and the American Political System* (Boston: Little, Brown and Company, 1983) v.

3. Walter Lippman, quoted in Barry B. Hughes, *The Domestic Context of American Foreign Policy* (San Francisco: W. H. Freeman and Company, 1978) 6.

4. Hans J. Morgenthau, quoted in Nathan and Oliver 159.

5. Nathan and Oliver 158.

6. Gabriel A. Almond, *The American People and Foreign Policy* (New York: Harcourt, Brace and Company, 1950) 4.

7. Gabriel Kolko, *The Roots of American Foreign Policy: An Analysis of Power and Purpose* (Boston: Beacon Press, 1969) 12–13.

8. Leslie H. Gelb and Richard K. Betts, *The Irony of Vietnam: The System Worked* (Washington DC: The Brookings Institution, 1979).

9. Robert P. Newman, "Lethal Rhetoric: The Selling of the China Myths," *Quarterly Journal of Speech* 61 (1975): 113–128.

10. Philip Wander, "The Rhetoric of American Foreign Policy," *Quarterly Journal of Speech* 70 (1984): 339–361; Walter R. Fisher, "Narration as a Human Communication Paradigm: The Case of Public Moral Argument," *Communication Monographs* 51 (1984): 1–21; G. Thomas Goodnight, "On Questions of Evacuation and Survival in Nuclear Conflict: A Case Study in Public Argument and Rhetorical Criticism," *Argument in Transition: Proceedings of the Third Summer Conference on Argu-*

mentation Ed. David Zarefsky (Annandale VA: Speech Communication Association, 1983) 319–338; G. Thomas Goodnight, "Ronald Reagan's Reformulation of the Rhetoric of War: Analysis of the 'Zero Option,' 'Evil Empire,' and 'Star Wars' Addresses," *Quarterly Journal of Speech* 72 (1986): 390–414.

11. Much has been written on the "nuclear priesthood" and their use of language and expertise to guide nuclear policy. See Richard Delgado, "The Language of the Arms Race: Should the People Limit Government Speech?" *Boston University Law Review* 64 (1984): 961–1001; Stephen Hilgartner, Richard C. Bell, and Rory O'Connor, *Nukespeak: Nuclear Language, Visions and Mindset* (San Francisco: Sierra Club Books, 1982).

12. Nathan and Oliver argue (183), for example, that there is no evidence to warrant the conclusion that the public is incapable of dealing with complex foreign policy information when it is provided.

13. Hughes 224.

14. Alexander Cockburn and James Ridgeway, "The Freeze Movement Versus Reagan," *New Left Review* 137 (1983): 7.

15. Richard K. Betts, "Nuclear Weapons," *The Making of America's Soviet Policy* ed. Joseph S. Nye, Jr. (New Haven: Yale University Press, 1984) 106.

16. Betts 101–102.

17. Robert L. Ivie, "Images of Savagery in American Justifications for War," *Communication Monographs* 47 (1980): 279–294.

18. Robert L. Ivie, "Speaking 'Common Sense' About the Soviet Threat: Reagan's Rhetorical Stance," *Western Journal of Speech Communication* 48 (1984): 39–50.

19. Robert L. Ivie, "Metaphor and the Rhetorical Invention of Cold War 'Idealists,'" *Communication Monographs* 54 (1987): 165–182.

20. Joseph S. Nye, Jr., "The Domestic Roots of American Foreign Policy," *The Making of America's Soviet Policy* 7.

21. Ivie, "Speaking 'Common Sense.'"

22. Writers in the Frankfurt School, particularly Jurgen Habermas, consider the ideological role that technology plays in the post-industrial

world. Jurgen Habermas, *Toward a Rational Society* (Boston: Beacon Press, 1970). See also David Held, *Introduction to Critical Theory: Horkheimer to Habermas* (Berkeley: University of California Press, 1980).

23. Fisher 15.

24. G. Thomas Goodnight, "The Personal, Technical and Public Spheres of Argument: A Speculative Inquiry into the Art of Public Deliberation," *Journal of the American Forensic Association* 18 (1982): 214–227.

25. Thomas B. Farrell and G. Thomas Goodnight, "Accidental Rhetoric: The Root Metaphors of Three Mile Island," *Communication Monographs* 48 (1981): 271–300.

26. Janice Hocker Rushing, "Ronald Reagan's 'Star Wars' Address: Mythic Containment of Technical Reasoning," *Quarterly Journal of Speech* 72 (1986): 415–433.

27. For an example of a scientific heretic, see Thomas M. Lessl, "Science and the Sacred Cosmos: The Ideological Rhetoric of Carl Sagan," *Quarterly Journal of Speech* 71 (1985): 175–187.

28. Kenneth Burke, "Definition of Man," *Language as Symbolic Action* (Berkeley: University of California Press, 1966) 16–24.

Works Cited

Adelman, Kenneth A. "Making Arms Control Work." *Department of State Bulletin* 86 (January 1986): 39–42.

———. "Star Wars in the Desert." *Newsweek* 4 February 1991: 14.

Adler, Selig. "The Isolationist Impulse." Stone 36–46.

"After the Patriot." *Wall Street Journal* 23 January 1991: A12.

Almond, Gabriel A. *The American People and Foreign Policy.* New York: Harcourt, Brace, and Company, 1950.

Andrews, James R. "They Chose the Sword: Appeals to War in Nineteenth-Century American Public Address." *Today's Speech* 17 (1969): 3–8.

Arkin, William M. "Gorbachev Talks But Who Listens?" *Bulletin of the Atomic Scientists* (March 1989): 5–6.

Ashley, Richard K. "Living on Border Lines: Man, Poststructuralism, and War." DerDerian and Shapiro 259–321.

Baker, James. "America's Stake in the Persian Gulf." *U. S. Department of State Dispatch* 10 September 1990: 69–71.

———. "From Points to Pathways of Mutual Advantage: Next Steps in Soviet–American Relations." *U. S. Department of State Dispatch* 22 October 1990: 199–203.

———. "Recent Developments in US–Soviet Relations." *U. S. Department of State Dispatch* 3 September 1990: 45–48.

———. "Remarks to U. S. Troops." *U. S. Department of State Dispatch* 12 November 1990: 260–261.

——. "The International Agenda and the FY 1990 Budget Request." *Department of State Bulletin* (April 1989): 16–21.

——. "U. S. Foreign Policy Priorities and the FY 1991 Budget." *U. S. Department of State Dispatch* 3 September 1990: 1–10.

——. "Why America is in the Gulf." *U. S. Department of State Dispatch* 5 November 1990: 235–237.

Barnes, Fred. "Pebbles Go Bam-Bam." *The New Republic* 17 April 1989: 12–15.

Bennett, W. Lance. *Public Opinion in American Politics.* New York: Harcourt Brace Jovanovich, 1980.

Bethe, Hans A. "Chop Down the Nuclear Arsenals." *Bulletin of the Atomic Scientists* (March 1989): 11–15.

Betts, Richard K. "Nuclear Weapons." Nye 97–127.

Blum, Deborah. "Wierd Science: Livermore's X-Ray Laser Flap." *Bulletin of the Atomic Scientists* (July/August 1988): 7–13.

Boffey, Philip M., et al. *Claiming the Heavens.* New York: Times Books, 1988.

Bormann, Ernest G. *The Force of Fantasy: Restoring the American Dream.* Carbondale, IL: Southern Illinois University Press, 1985.

Bowers, Claude G. *Beveridge and the Progressive Era.* New York: The Literary Guild, 1932.

Boyer, Paul. *By the Bomb's Early Light.* New York: Pantheon Books, 1985.

——. "From Activism to Apathy: The American People and Nuclear Weapons, 1963–1980." *The Journal of American History* 70 (1984): 821–844.

Boyte, Harry C. "The Foundation of the New Peace Movement: A Communitarian Perspective." *Social Policy* 13 (1982): 4–8.

Brockriede, Wayne, and Robert L. Scott. *Moments in the Rhetoric of the Cold War.* New York: Random House, 1970.

Brummett, Barry. "Perfection and the Bomb: Nuclear Weapons, Teleology, and Motives." *Journal of Communication* 39 (Winter 1989): 85–95.

Bundy, McGeorge, et. al. "The President's Choice: Star Wars or Arms Control." *Foreign Affairs* 63 (Winter 1984/85): 264–278.

Burke, Kenneth. *A Grammar of Motives*. Berkeley: University of California Press, 1969.

———. *A Rhetoric of Motives*. Berkeley: University of California Press, 1969.

———. "Definition of Man." *Language as Symbolic Action* 3–24.

———. "Dramatism." *Drama in Life: The Uses of Communication in Society*. Eds. James E. Combs and Michael W. Mansfield. New York: Hastings House Publishers, 1976. 7–17.

———. *Language as Symbolic Action*. Berkeley: University of California Press, 1966.

———. *Permanence and Change*. Berkeley: University of California Press, 1984.

Burrows, William E. "Ballistic Missile Defense: The Illusion of Security." *Foreign Affairs* 62 (1984): 843–856.

Burt, Richard. "Nuclear and Space Talks Open Round Eleven." *Department of State Bulletin* (August 1989): 73–74.

Bush, George. "Against Aggression in the Persian Gulf." *U. S. Department of State Dispatch* 3 September 1990: 54–55.

———. "America's Stand Against Aggression." *U. S. Department of State Dispatch* 3 September 1990: 55+.

———. "Change in the Soviet Union." *Department of State Bulletin* (July 1989): 16–17.

———. "Remarks to U. S. Troops." *U. S. Department of State Dispatch* 12 November 1990: 260–261.

———. "Security Strategy for the 1990s." *Department of State Bulletin* (July 1989): 19–21.

———. "State of the Union Address." *U. S. Department of State Dispatch* 4 February 1991: 65+.

———. "Thanksgiving Day Address to US Forces in Saudi Arabia." *U. S. Department of State Dispatch* 26 November 1990: 279–280.

———. "The Arabian Peninsula: U. S. Principles." *U. S. Department of State Dispatch* 3 September 1990: 52–53.

————. "The UN: World Parliament of Peace." *U. S. Department of State Dispatch* 8 October 1990: 151–153.

————. "Toward a New World Order." *U. S. Department of State Dispatch* 17 September 1990: 91+.

"Bush May Keep Midgetman Despite Cheney." *Salt Lake Tribune* 22 April 1989: A1–2.

Caldicott, Helen. "A Commitment to Life." *The Humanist* September–October 1982: 5–11.

————. *Missile Envy: The Arms Race and Nuclear War.* New York: Bantam Books, 1985.

Carlson, A. Cheree. "Albert J. Beveridge as Imperialist and Progressive: The Means Justify the Ends." *Western Journal of Speech Communication* 52 (1988): 46–62.

Carter, Ashton B. "Directed Energy Missile Defense in Space: Background Paper." *Strategic Defense and Anti-Satellite Weapons* 259–338.

Cassata, Donna. "Senate OK's $289 Billion Defense Bill." *Salt Lake Tribune* 5 August 1990: A1–2.

Chapman, Gary. "Smart Rocks, Brilliant Pebbles, Genius Dust." *Bulletin of the Atomic Scientists* (November 1989): 10+.

Cherwitz, Richard A. "Lyndon Johnson and the 'Crisis' of Tonkin Gulf: A President's Justification of War." *Western Journal of Speech Communication* 42 (1978): 93–104.

Chernus, Ira. *Dr. Strangegod: On the Symbolic Meaning of Nuclear Weapons.* Columbia: University of South Carolina Press, 1986.

Cimbala, Stephen J. *Rethinking Nuclear Strategy.* Wilmington, Delaware: Scholarly Resources, Inc., 1988.

————. ed. *The Technology, Strategy and Politics of SDI.* Boulder: Westview Press, 1987.

Clark, E. Culpepper. "Argument and Historical Analysis." Cox and Willard 298–317.

Cockburn, Alexander, and James Ridgeway. "The Freeze Movement Versus Reagan." *New Left Review* 137 (1983): 5–21.

Cohn, Carol. "Sex and Death in the Rational World of Defense Intellectuals." *Signs: Journal of Women in Culture and Society* 12 (1987): 687–718.

Cole, Paul M. "The Reagan administration's Reaction to the Nuclear Weapons Freeze Movement." Cole and Taylor 93–106.

Cole, Paul M., and William J. Taylor, eds. *The Nuclear Freeze Debate: Arms Control Issues for the 1980s.* Boulder: Westview Press, 1983.

"Conference Fallout." *Bulletin of the Atomic Scientists* (December 1990): 4.

Cooper, Henry F. "Status of the Defense and Space Talks." *Department of State Bulletin* (October 1989): 20–22.

Cox, Robert J., and Charles Arthur Willard, eds. *Advances in Argumentation Theory and Research.* Carbondale: Southern Illinois University Press, 1982.

David, Charles-Philippe. *Debating Counterforce.* Boulder, CO: Westview Press, 1987.

Davidson, Donald L. *Nuclear Weapons and the American Churches: Ethical Positions on Modern Warfare.* Boulder: Westview Press, 1983.

Delgado, Richard. "The Language of the Arms Race: Should the People Limit Government Speech?" *Boston University Law Review* 64 (1984): 961–1001.

Department of Defense. "Strategic Defense Initiative." *Department of State Bulletin* 84 (May 1984): 71–72.

Der Derian, James. "The Boundaries of Knowledge and Power in International Relations." Der Derian and Shapiro 3–10.

Der Derian, James, and Michael J. Shapiro. *International/Intertextual Relations: Postmodern Readings of World Politics.* Lexington, MA: Lexington Books, 1989.

Derrida, Jacques. "No Apocalypse, Not Now (full speed ahead, seven missiles, seven missives)." *Diacritics* (Summer 1984): 20–31.

Drinan, Robert F. *Beyond the Nuclear Freeze.* New York: The Seabury Press, 1983.

Duncan, Hugh Dalziel. Introduction. *Permanence and Change.* By Kenneth Burke. Berkeley: University of California Press, 1984.

Dunn, Marcia. "New SDI: Icing on Stale Cake or Savior for U. S. Defense?" *Salt Lake Tribune* 31 March 1991: A8.

Editorials on File. 13 (August 1–15, 1982): 875.

Editorials on File. 13 (June 1–15, 1982): 646.

Editorials on File. 13 (March 16–31, 1982): 306+.

Etzold, Thomas H., and John Lewis Gaddis, eds. *Containment: Documents on American Policy and Strategy, 1945–1950.* New York: Columbia University Press, 1978.

Farrell, Thomas B., and G. Thomas Goodnight. "Accidental Rhetoric: The Root Metaphors of Three Mile Island." *Communication Monographs* 48 (1981): 271–300.

Farrell, Thomas B. "Knowledge, Consensus, and Rhetorical Theory." *Quarterly Journal of Speech* 62 (1976): 1–14.

———. "Social Knowledge II." *Quarterly Journal of Speech* 64 (1978): 329–334.

Feighan, Edward F. "The Freeze in Congress." Cole and Taylor 29–55.

Feld, Bernard T. "A Mutual Freeze." *Bulletin of the Atomic Scientists* 38 (May 1982): 2–3.

Fisher, Walter R. *Human Communication as Narration: Toward a Philosophy of Reason, Value, and Action.* Columbia: University of South Carolina Press, 1987.

———. "Narration as a Human Communication Paradigm: The Case of Public Moral Argument." *Communication Monographs* 51 (1984): 1–21.

Fisher, Walter R., and Richard Dean Burns, eds. *Armament and Disarmament: The Continuing Dispute.* Belmont, CA: Wadsworth, 1964.

Gaddis, John Lewis. *Strategies of Containment.* New York: Oxford University Press, 1982.

———. *The United States and the Origins of the Cold War 1941–1947.* New York: Columbia University Press, 1972.

Gardner, Lloyd C., Walter F. LaFeber, and Thomas J. McCormick. *Creation of the American Empire.* Chicago: Rand McNally, 1973.

Garfinkle, Adam M. *The Politics of the Nuclear Freeze.* Philadelphia: Foreign Policy Research Institute, 1984.

Garn, Jake. "Should the U. S. Now Negotiate an 'In-Place' Freeze on Nuclear Weapons?" *Congressional Digest* 61 (August–September 1982): 215–217.

Gelb, Leslie H., and Richard K. Betts. *The Irony of Vietnam: The System Worked.* Washington: The Brookings Institution, 1979.

Geneste, Marc. "Strategic Defense and the Shield of Europe." *Strategic Review* 13 (Spring 1985): 37–43.

Gianakos, Perry E., and Albert Karson, eds. *The World Arena.* Vol 2 of *American Diplomacy and the Sense of Destiny.* 4 vols. Belmont, CA: Wadsworth Publishing Company, 1966.

Glaser, Charles L. "Do we Want the Missile Defenses We Can Build?" *International Security* 10 (Summer 1985): 25–57.

Goldberg, Robert A. *Grassroots Resistance: Social Movements in Twentieth Century America.* Belmont, CA: Wadsworth, 1991.

Goldzwig, Steve, and George Cheney. "The U. S. Catholic Bishops on Nuclear Arms: Corporate Advocacy, Role Redefinition, and Rhetorical Adaptation." *Central States Speech Journal* 35 (1984): 8–23.

Goodnight, G. Thomas. "On Questions of Evacuation and Survival in Nuclear Conflict: A Case Study in Public Argument and Rhetorical Criticism." *Argument in Transition: Proceedings of the Third Summer Conference on Argumentation.* Eds. David Zarefsky, Malcolm Sillars and Jack Rhodes. Annandale, VA: Speech Communication Association, 1983. 319–338.

————. "Ronald Reagan's Re-formulation of the Rhetoric of War: Analysis of the 'Zero Option,' 'Evil Empire,' and 'Star Wars' Addresses." *Quarterly Journal of Speech* 72 (1986): 390–414.

————. "The Personal, Technical, and Public Spheres of Argument: A Speculative Inquiry Into the Art of Public Deliberation." *Journal of the American Forensic Association* 18 (1982): 214–227.

Graebner, Norman A. *America as a World Power: A Realist Appraisal from Wilson to Reagan.* Wilmington: Scholarly Resources, Inc. 1984.

Griffin, Leland. "A Dramatistic Theory of the Rhetoric of Movements." Rueckert 456–478.

Guerrier, Steven W. & Wayne C. Thompson, eds. *Perspectives on Strategic Defense*. Boulder: Westview Press, 1987.

Habermas, Jurgen. *Toward a Rational Society*. Boston: Beacon Press, 1970.

Halliday, Fred. *The Making of the Second Cold War*. London: Verso Editions, 1986.

Halloran, Richard. "As Pentagon Budget Unfolds, Space Missile Shield is Intact." *New York Times* 2 March 1989: B11.

Harding, Samuel Bannister, ed. *Select Orations Illustrating American Political History*. New York: Macmillan, 1919.

Harris, Louis. "Public Opinion and the Freeze Movement." *The Nuclear Weapons Freeze and Arms Control* 39–40.

Hart, James L. "The Case for a Freeze On Nuclear Arms." *America* 23 October 1982: 226–228.

Hatfield, Mark O. "Should the U. S. Now Negotiate an 'In-Place' Freeze on Nuclear Weapons?" *Congressional Digest* 61 (August–September 1982): 208–214.

Held, David. *Introduction to Critical Theory: Horkheimer to Habermas*. Berkeley: University of California Press, 1980.

Henry, David. "Idealism vs. Realism: Campaign Rhetoric in the Scientists' Movement, 1945–1962." Paper presented at the Annual Meeting of the Western Speech Communication Association, San Diego, CA, February, 1988.

Hikins, James W. "The Rhetoric of 'Unconditional Surrender' and the Decision to Drop the Atomic Bomb." *Quarterly Journal of Speech* 69 (1983): 379–400.

Hilgartner, Stephen, et al. *Nukespeak: Nuclear Language, Visions and Mindset*. San Francisco: Sierra Club Books, 1982.

Hoffman, Fred S. "Ballistic Missile Defenses and U. S. National Security." *Strategic Defense and Anti-Satellite Weapons* 125–140.

———. "The SDI in U. S. Nuclear Strategy." *International Security* 10 (Summer 1985): 13–24.

Hogan, J. Michael. "Apocalyptic Pornography and the Nuclear Freeze: A Defense of the Public." *Argument and Critical Practices*. Ed. Joseph W. Wenzel. Annandale, VA: Speech Communication Association, 1987.

————. "Public Opinion and American Foreign Policy: The Case of Illusory Support for the Panama Canal Treaties." *Quarterly Journal of Speech* 71 (1985): 302–317.

Hollenbach, David. *Nuclear Ethics: A Christian Moral Argument.* New York: Paulist Press, 1983.

Hollihan, Thomas A. "The Public Controversy Over the Panama Canal Treaties: An Analysis of American Foreign Policy Rhetoric." *Western Journal of Speech Communication* 50 (1986): 368–387.

Holt, W. Stull. "Playing Politics With the League." Stone 27–35.

Hughes, Barry B. *The Domestic Context of American Foreign Policy.* San Francisco: W. H. Freeman and Company, 1978.

Huntington, Samuel P. "American Ideals versus American Institutions." *Political Science Quarterly* 97 (1982): 1–37.

Ivie, Robert L. "Images of Savagery in American Justifications for War." *Communication Monographs* 47 (1980): 279–294.

————. "Metaphor and the Rhetorical Invention of Cold War 'Idealists.'" *Communication Monographs* 54 (1987): 165–182.

————. "Presidential Motives for War." *Quarterly Journal of Speech* 60 (1974): 337–345.

————. "Speaking 'Common Sense' About the Soviet Threat: Reagan's Rhetorical Stance." *Western Journal of Speech Communication* 48 (1984): 39–50.

————. "The Metaphor of Force in Pro-War Discourse: The Case of 1812." *Quarterly Journal of Speech* 68 (1982): 240–253.

Jan Mohamed, Abdul. "The Economy of Manichean Allegory: The Function of Racial Difference in Colonialist Literature." *Critical Inquiry* 12 (Autumn 1985): 59–87.

Jasani, Bhupendra, ed. *Space Weapons and International Security.* Oxford: Oxford University Press, 1987.

Kahan, Jerome H. *Security in the Nuclear Age.* Washington: The Brookings Institution, 1975.

Kalicki, Jan H. "Arms Control and the Nuclear Weapons Freeze." *The Nuclear Weapons Freeze and Arms Control* 13–17.

Kaltefleiter, Werner. "Strategic Defense on the Broader Historical Stage." *Strategic Review* 13 (Summer 1985): 14–21.

Kane, Francis X., et. al. "Strategic Defenses and Deterrence: A Strategic-Operational Assessment." *Strategic Review* 17 (Winter 1989): 41–54.

Kennedy, Edward M. "Nuclear Weapons Freeze Proposal Followed by Major Reductions in the Nuclear Arsenals." *Bulletin of Peace Proposals* 13 (1982): 249–252.

Kennedy, Edward M., and Mark O. Hatfield. *Freeze! How You Can Help Prevent Nuclear War.* New York: Bantam Books, 1982.

Klein, Bradley S. "The Textual Strategies of the Military: Or Have You Read Any Good Defense Manuals Lately?" Der Derian and Shapiro 97–112.

Kolko, Gabriel. *The Roots of American Foreign Policy: An Analysis of Power and Purpose.* Boston: Beacon Press, 1969.

Krepon, Michael. "Don't Parrot Old Arguments on Missile Defense." *Bulletin of the Atomic Scientists* (January–February 1991): 12–13.

Lake, Randall A. "Order and Disorder in Anti-Abortion Rhetoric: A Logological View." *Quarterly Journal of Speech* 70 (1984): 425–443.

Lapidus, Gail W., and Alexander Dallin. "The Pacification of Ronald Reagan." *Bulletin of the Atomic Scientists* (January/February 1989): 14–17.

Leary, Mary Ellen. "Nuclear Freeze: Bishops and Nobel Laureates." *Commonweal* 29 (January 1982): 39–41.

Lehman, Christopher M. "Arms Control vs the Freeze." *The Nuclear Weapons Freeze and Arms Control* 65–71.

Lessl, Thomas M. "Science and the Sacred Cosmos: The Ideological Rhetoric of Carl Sagan." *Quarterly Journal of Speech* 71 (1985): 175–187.

Link, Arthur S. *1897–1920.* Vol. 1 of *American Epoch: A History of the United States Since the 1890s.* 3 vols. New York: Alfred A. Knopf, 1967.

———. *Campaigns for Progressivism and Peace.* Vol. 5 of *Wilson.* 5 vols. Princeton: Princeton University Press, 1965.

———. *The Impact of World War I.* New York: Harper and Row, 1969.

Luke, Timothy W. "'What's Wrong With Deterrence?' A Semiotic Interpretation of National Security Policy." Der Derian and Shapiro 207–229.

Mandelbaum, Michael, and Strobe Talbott. *Reagan and Gorbachev.* New York: Vintage Books, 1987.

May, Ernest R. *The Making of the Monroe Doctrine.* Cambridge: Harvard University Press, 1975.

McCormick, James M. *American Foreign Policy and American Values.* Itasca, IL: F. E. Peacock Publishers, 1985.

McCormick, Richard A. "Nuclear Deterrence and the Problem of Intention: A Review of the Positions." Murnion 168–182.

McGee, Michael Calvin. "'Social Movement': Phenomenon or Meaning?" *Central States Speech Journal* 31 (1980): 233–244.

Mechling, Elizabeth Walker, and Jay Mechling. "The Campaign for Civil Defense and the Struggle to Naturalize the Bomb." *Western Journal of Speech Communication* 55 (1991): 105–133.

Mendelsohn, Jack. "The Freeze Movement as an Ethical Achievement." *The Nuclear Weapons Freeze and Arms Control* 100–102.

Miller, Steven E. & Steven VanEvera, eds. *The Star Wars Controversy.* Princeton: Princeton University Press, 1986.

Morain, Dan. "Energy Secretary Warns Weapons Scientists Not to Disagree in Public." *Los Angeles Times* 23 July 1988, Part I: 24.

Morgenthau, Hans J. *The Purpose of American Politics.* New York: Alfred A. Knopf, 1960.

Murnion, Philip J., ed. *Catholics and Nuclear War.* New York: Crossroad Publishing Company, 1983.

Nathan, James A., and James K. Oliver. *Foreign Policy Making and the American Political System.* Boston: Little, Brown and Company, 1983.

National Council of Catholic Bishops. "The Challenge of Peace: God's Promise and Our Response." Murnion 245–338.

Newman, Robert P. "Lethal Rhetoric: The Selling of the China Myths." *Quarterly Journal of Speech* 61 (1975): 113–128.

Niebuhr, Reinhold. *The Irony of American History.* New York: Charles Scribner's Sons, 1952.

Nitze, Paul H. "SDI, Arms Control, and Stability: Toward a New Synthesis." *Department of State Bulletin* 86 (August 1986): 44–46.

———. "SDI: The Soviet Program." *Department of State Bulletin* 85 (September 1985): 40–42.

Nitze, Paul H., and Abraham D. Sofaer. "The ABM Treaty and the SDI Program." *Department of State Bulletin* 85 (December 1985): 37–40.

Norman, Colin. "SDI Heads for Fiscal Crash." *Science* 247 (16 March 1990): 1283–1285.

The Nuclear Weapons Freeze and Arms Control. Proceedings of a Symposium held at the American Academy of Arts and Sciences. January 13–15, 1983. Cambridge: President and Fellows of Harvard College, 1983.

Nye, Joseph S., ed. *The Making of America's Soviet Policy.* New Haven: Yale University Press, 1984.

Paine, Christopher E. "Conceptual Foundations of a Comprehensive Nuclear Freeze." *The Nuclear Weapons Freeze and Arms Control* 25–30.

Payne, Keith B. *Missile Defense in the 21st Century: Protection Against Limited Threats.* Boulder: Westview Press, 1991.

Payne, Keith B. & Colin S. Gray, "Nuclear Policy and the Defensive Transition." *Foreign Affairs* 62 (1984): 820–842.

Peffer, Nathaniel. "Politics Is Peace." *The American Scholar* 15 (April 1946): 160–166.

Pike, John. "Qaddafi Goes Ballistic." *The New Republic* 20 March 1989: 14–16.

Potter, Ralph B. *War and Moral Discourse.* Richmond: John Knox Press, 1969.

Procter, David E. "The Rescue Mission: Assigning Guilt to a Chaotic Scene." *Western Journal of Speech Communication* 51 (1987): 245–255.

Quayle, Dan. "America's Objectives in the Persian Gulf." *U. S. Department of State Dispatch* 10 December 1990: 310–312.

Reagan, Ronald. "President Reagan's Address to the Nation, December 10, 1987." *Department of State Bulletin* 88 (February 1988): 18–21.

Reid, Ronald F. "New England Rhetoric and the French War, 1754–1760: A Case Study in the Rhetoric of War." *Communication Monographs* 43 (1976): 259–286.

Ridenour, Louis N. "Science and Secrecy." *The American Scholar* 15 (April 1946): 147–153.

Rivkin, David B. Jr. "SDI: Strategic Reality or Never-Never Land?" *Strategic Review* 15 (Summer 1987): 43–54.

Robertson, James Oliver. *American Myths, American Reality.* New York: Hill and Wang, 1980.

Rosenthal, Andrew. "Tower Declares 'Star Wars' Shield Can't Be Complete." *New York Times* 27 January 1989: A1+

Rueckert, William, ed. *Critical Responses to Kenneth Burke.* Minneapolis: University of Minnesota Press, 1969.

Rushing, Janice Hocker. "Ronald Reagan's 'Star Wars' Address: Mythic Containment of Technical Reasoning." *Quarterly Journal of Speech* 72 (1986): 415–433.

Said, Edward W. *Orientalism.* New York: Vintage Books, 1979.

———. "Representing the Colonized: Anthropology's Interlocutors." *Critical Inquiry* 15 (Winter 1989): 205–225.

Scheer, Robert. "Scientists Split Over 'Star Wars.'" *Los Angeles Times* 24 September 1985, Sec. I: 1+.

———. "'Star Wars': A Program in Disarray." *Los Angeles Times* 22 September 1985: 1+.

———. "The Man Who Blew the Whistle on 'Star Wars.'" *Los Angeles Times Magazine* 17 July 1988: 6+.

———. *With Enough Shovels: Reagan, Bush and Nuclear War.* New York: Random House, 1982.

Schell, Jonathan. *The Fate of the Earth.* New York: Alfred A. Knopf, 1982.

Schlesinger, James R. "Rhetoric and Realities in the Star Wars Debate." *International Security* 10 (Summer 1985): 3–12.

Schmitt, Eric. "House Approves Military Budget, Cutting B–2 and 'Star Wars.'" *New York Times* 23 May 1991: A1–C18.

Schultz, George. "Reykjavik: A Watershed in U. S.–Soviet Relations." *Department of State Bulletin* 86 (December 1986): 22–25.

———. "Secretary's Interview on 'Face the Nation.'" *Department of State Bulletin* 88 (January 1988): 7–9.

Shapiro, Michael J. "Textualizing Global Politics." Der Derian and Shapiro 11–22.

Simons, Herbert W., Elizabeth W. Mechling, and Howard N. Schrier. "The Functions of Human Communication in Mobilizing for Action from the Bottom Up: The Rhetoric of Social Movements." Carroll C. Arnold and John Waite Bowers, eds. *Handbook on Rhetorical and Communication Theory.* Boston: Allyn and Bacon, 1984–1985: 792–867.

Slater, Jerome & David Goldfischer. "Can SDI Provide a Defense?" *Political Science Quarterly* 101 (1986): 839–856.

Sloss, Leon. "The Return of Strategic Defense." *Strategic Review* 12 (Summer 1984): 37–44.

Smith, F. Michael. "Rhetorical Implications of the 'Aggression' Thesis in the Johnson Administration's Vietnam Argumentation." *Central States Speech Journal* 23 (1972): 217–224.

Smith, R. Jeffrey. "Weapons Bureaucracy Spurns Star Wars Goal." *Strategic Defense and Anti-Satellite Weapons* 52–55.

Spaeth, Robert L. *No Easy Answers: Christians Debate Nuclear Arms.* Minneapolis: Winston Press, 1983.

Spanier, John. *American Foreign Policy Since World War II.* New York: Holt, Rinehart and Winston, 1983.

Spurlin, Paul Merrill. *The French Enlightenment in America.* Athens: University of Georgia Press, 1984.

Steel, Ronald. *Walter Lippman and the American Century.* New York: Vintage Books, 1980.

Stewart, Charles, Craig Smith, and Robert E. Denton. *Persuasion and Social Movements.* Prospect Heights, IL: Waveland Press, 1984.

Stone, Ralph A., ed. *Wilson and the League of Nations.* New York: Holt, Rinehart and Winston, 1967.

Stourzh, Gerald. *Benjamin Franklin and American Foreign Policy.* Chicago: University of Chicago Press, 1969.

Thompson, Mark. "Command System, High-Tech Weapons Win High Marks." *Salt Lake Tribune* 10 March 1991: 4A.

"Too Brilliant By Half." *The New Republic* 29 May 1989: 7–9.

Tuchman, Barbara W. *The Guns of August.* New York: Macmillan, 1962.

Tucker, Robert W. *A New Isolationism: Threat or Promise?* New York: Universe Books, 1972.

United States. Congress. House. Committee on Armed Services. *Strategic Defense Initiative (SDI) Program.* 99th Cong., 1st sess. Washington: GPO, 1985.

United States. Congress. House. Subcommittee of the Committee on Government Operations. *Cost Estimates for Phase I of the Strategic Defense Initiative.* 101st Cong., 1st Sess. Washington: GPO, 1989.

United States. Congress. Senate. Committee on Appropriations. *Department of Defense Authorization for Appropriations for Fiscal Year 1986.* 99th Cong., 1st sess. Washington: GPO, 1985.

United States. Congress. Senate. Committee on Appropriations. *Department of Defense Authorization for Appropriations for Fiscal Years 1988 & 1989.* 100th Cong., 1st sess. Washington: GPO, 1987.

United States. Congress. Senate. Committee on Foreign Relations. *Strategic Defense and Anti-Satellite Weapons.* 98th Cong., 2nd sess. Washington: GPO, 1984.

United States. Department of Defense. "Defense Against Ballistic Missiles: An Assessment of Technologies and Policy Implications." *Strategic Defense and Anti-Satellite Weapons* 94–124.

United States. Office of Technology Assessment. *The Effects of Nuclear War.* Washington: GPO, 1979.

United States. Office of the Federal Register. *Weekly Compilation of Presidential Documents.* Washington: GPO.

United States. *The President's Strategic Defense Initiative.* Washington: The President, 1985.

Waller, Douglas C. "The Impact of the Nuclear Freeze Movement on Congress." *The Nuclear Weapons Freeze and Arms Control* 47–52.

Wander, Philip. "The Rhetoric of American Foreign Policy." *Quarterly Journal of Speech* 70 (1984): 339–361.

Washington, George. "Farewell Address." Harding 150–163.

Weigley, Russell F. *The American Way of War.* New York: Macmillan, 1973.

Weisman, Steven R. "Reagan Says Plan on Missile Defense Will Prevent War." *New York Times* 26 March 1983: 1+.

Williams, David Cratis. "Nuclear Criticism: In Pursuit of a 'Politically Enabling' Deconstructive Voice." *Journal of the American Forensic Association* 14 (1988): 193–205.

Index

Abrahamson, Lt. Gen. James A., 71, 76, 86, 88
Accidental Launch Protection System (ALPS), 105–106
Action. See Burke, Kenneth
Adelman, Kenneth, 72, 106
Agency. See Burke, Kenneth
Agent. See Burke, Kenneth
Almond, Gabriel, 117
Antiballistic Missile (ABM) Treaty, 77, 85–86, 93
Antinuclear movement, 11, 17, 39, 44, 45. See also Nuclear freeze campaign
Arms control, 51, 56–57. See also Nuclear disarmament; Nuclear freeze campaign
Ashley, Richard K., 22
Aspin, Les, 94

Baker, James, 94–95, 98, 102–103, 105, 110
Ball, George, 55
Ballistic missile defense. See Strategic Defense Initiative
Bethe, Hans, 94
Betts, Richard, 118, 121
Beveridge, Albert J., 29
Biden, Joseph, 87
Boxer, Barbara, 96

Boyer, Paul, 15, 43, 44, 45
Brilliant pebbles, 95–96, 113, 154n.19
Burke, Kenneth, 4, 38, 67, 82–83; action, 67, 83, 108, 129; dramatism, 9–12, 50, 81–84; guilt, 38, 82–84, 101, 129; hierarchy, 10, 38, 50, 82–84, 101–102, 108, 110, 113, 125, 129; motion, 18, 66, 67, 83, 129; motive, 11–12; ontological assumptions of, 10; order, 11, 38, 50, 60, 123; pentad, 11–12, 66–73; perfection, 10, 60, 82–84, 124, 129, 131; scapegoat, 124; transcendence, 66, 68–69, 73, 83–84, 91–92, 102–104, 113, 129; worldview, 11. See also Language; Rhetoric; Symbols
Burt, Richard, 93
Bush, George: administration of, 9, 18, 19; and new world order, 37–38, 97–104; and Persian Gulf War (1991), 97–104, 115; and SDI, 91–107; early attitudes toward SDI, 92–93; rhetoric of, 91–92, 98–104, 110, 130

Caldicott, Helen, 52–54
Carter, Jimmy, 37, 41, 46, 121
Catholic Church. See National Council of Catholic Bishops
Cheney, Dick, 106, 110

Chernus, Ira, 4–5, 14
Civil defense, 45, 47
Cold war, 14, 45, 117; collapse of, 19,
    91, 95–98, 102, 112; rhetoric of,
    36–37, 76, 94, 99, 111, 123–124;
    SDI and the end of, 92–97, 104–113
Colonialism, 108–110; and dualism,
    111; and hegemony, 108–109,
    110–113; and ideology, 108–109,
    110–113, 130; and rhetoric,
    108–110, 130
Commager, Henry Steele, 25
Cooper, Henry F., 93, 106
Cooper, Robert S., 86–88
Counterforce, 48, 55, 58–59, 62,
    144n.16

David, Charles-Philippe, 46
Derrida, Jacques, 3
Destiny: America's sense of, 18–19, 22,
    23–25, 28–29, 30, 33–38, 97, 113,
    129; and technology, 116; Persian
    Gulf War and America's sense of,
    91; SDI and America's sense of, 65,
    71–75, 115. See also Mission;
    Moralism in U. S. foreign policy
de Tocqueville, Alexis, 116–117
Deterrence, 3, 15, 43, 46, 54, 58–60, 62,
    79–81, 127. See also Mutual Assured
    Destruction
Discourse. See Language; Rhetoric;
    Symbols
Dramatism. See Burke, Kenneth
Drinan, Robert, 51
Dualism in foreign policy rhetoric,
    6–7, 36, 98–104, 110–112, 122–125,
    130–131
Duncan, Hugh Dalziel, 4

Eisenhower, Dwight D., 13, 37
Enemy images, 5–6, 92, 99–104,
    107–113, 123. See also Dualism in
    foreign policy rhetoric

Farrell, Thomas B., 126
Feld, Bernard, 51
Fisher, Walter R., 7, 125–126
Forsberg, Randall, 15–16, 48
Fosdick, Harry Emerson, 44
Franklin, Benjamin, 25, 27
Frontier: technology as new, 24, 65,
    71–72, 115, 127; western, 24, 27–28

Gardner, John, 72
Gardner, Lloyd, 24
Gelb, Leslie, 118
Global Protection Against Limited
    Strikes (GPALS), 92, 104, 110–111,
    113.
Globalism, 22, 32–33, 37. See also
    Internationalism; Isolationism
Goodnight, G. Thomas, 7, 8, 9, 126
Graebner, Norman, 30, 32, 34
Griffin, Leland, 50
Guilt. See Burke, Kenneth

Hatfield, Mark, 51–55, 57
Hegemony, 108, 112–113; and colo-
    nialism, 108–113; and ideology, 92,
    107, 110–113; and language,
    108–113, 123
Hierarchy. See Burke, Kenneth
Hikins, James, 35
Hiroshima, 8, 35, 42–43, 44, 54
Hitler, Adolph, 35. See also Hussein,
    Saddam, as new Hitler; World War
    II
Hoffman, Fred S., 88
Holt, W. Stull, 34
Hughes, Charles Evans, 31–32
Hussein, Saddam, 98–102, 110; as new
    "evil empire," 19, 91; as new Hitler,
    21, 99–100; as savage, 107–113, 115,
    123, 125; as uncivilized, 111–113,
    115. See also Persian Gulf War
    (1991)

Ideology: and America's sense of mission, 28, 36; and colonialism, 92, 108–113, 130; and hegemony, 92, 107; and rhetoric, 6, 22, 92, 110, 130
Imperialism, 29. *See also* Colonialism
Innocence: America's sense of, 38, 122; and SDI, 74, 81–84, 122; pre-nuclear, 39, 66, 83–84, 104; pre-symbolic, 66, 81–84
Internationalism, 31–32, 34. *See also* Globalism; Isolationism
Iraq, 111, 125; invasion of Kuwait, 97–104, 111. *See also* Hussein, Saddam; Persian Gulf War (1991)
Isolationism, 22, 30–34, 36. *See also* Globalism; Internationalism
Ivie, Robert L., 5, 123, 124

Jan Mohamed, Abdul, 109, 111
Jefferson, Thomas, 24–25, 27, 28

Kehler, Randy, 51
Kennan, George, 36
Kennedy, Edward, 52–57, 61
Kennedy, John F., 13
Keyworth, George A., 71–72
Kissinger, Henry, 37
Kolko, Gabriel, 117
Kuwait: invasion of, 97–104

LaFeber, Walter, 24
Language: and colonialism, 108–110, 123; and dramatism, 9–10; and technology, 10, 18, 38, 82–84, 125–130; and U. S. foreign policy, 2, 5–6; as action, 10, 67, 108; functions of, 1, 4, 11, 38, 81–82, 109; negative implications of, 66. *See also* Burke, Kenneth; Rhetoric; Symbols; U. S. foreign policy, as discursive
League of Nations, 32–34

Leary, Mary Ellen, 51
Limited nuclear war, 46–47, 121
Link, Arthur, 32
Lippman, Walter, 117
Luke, Timothy W., 3

McCormick, James, 35
McCormick, Thomas, 24
McNamara, Robert, 13
Meaning. *See* Language; Rhetoric; Symbols
Mendelsohn, Jack, 51, 54
Mission: America's sense of, 5, 7, 18, 21, 23–26, 28, 30, 33, 35–36, 97; Persian Gulf War (1991) and America's sense of, 91, 101; SDI and America's sense of, 65, 115. *See also* Destiny; Moralism in U. S. foreign policy
Monahan, Lt. Gen. George L., 96
Monroe Doctrine, 27–28
Moralism in U. S. foreign policy, 21–22, 26, 33, 35, 65–66. *See also* Destiny; Mission
Morgenthau, Hans, 22–23, 24, 38, 117
Motion. *See* Burke, Kenneth
Motive. *See* Burke, Kenneth
Mutual Assured Destruction (MAD), 1, 13, 17, 43, 62–63, 137n.41, 144n.16; logic of, 13, 14, 80–81; Reagan's rejection of, 67, 76, 80; SDI as replacement for, 69. *See also* Deterrence

Nagasaki, 35, 42–43, 44, 54
National Council of Catholic Bishops: Pastoral Letter on War and Peace, 41, 58–63
Neutrality, 29–35
New world order, 37, 91, 97, 102–104, 113
Newman, Robert P., 118
Niebuhr, Reinhold, 23, 38

Nixon, Richard M., 37
North-South relations, 107–113
Nuclear arms race, 2, 18, 39, 56; fear of, 62, 67, 69; morality of, 58; response by organized religion to, 57–60
Nuclear disarmament, 18, 48, 54, 66, 94. *See also* Nuclear freeze campaign
Nuclear freeze campaign, 15–18, 41, 45, 47, 115, 120–122, 138n.56; and arms control, 56–57, 77–78; common sense theme of, 50–52, 75–76; emotionalism in, 51–52; fear theme of, 52–53, 76–77; impatience theme of, 56–57; in Congress, 16, 49, 51; organizing strategy of, 48–49, 63; overkill theme of, 53–54, 77–78; rhetoric of, 42, 49–57, 75–81; rhetorical vulnerability of, 60–64, 75–81; role of organized religion in, 58; SDI as response to, 66, 75–81; support for, 16, 49, 56, 60; urgency theme of, 55–56
Nuclear proliferation, 2, 18, 19, 66, 77, 91, 97, 102, 105–107, 109–113, 115, 128, 131
Nuclear war: fear of, 52, 66, 68, 131; symbolic nature of, 3, 9, 81–82
Nuclear weapons: early reactions to, 42–45; guilt over, 38, 129; morality of use of, 44, 59; symbolic nature of, 4–5, 9; use of against Japan, 42–43
Nunn, Sam, 96, 105

Order. *See* Burke, Kenneth

Paine, Christopher, 56
Patriot missile, 18, 105–107
Payne, Keith, 107, 110, 111, 112–113
Peffer, Nathaniel, 43
Pentad. *See* Burke, Kenneth
Perfection. *See* Burke, Kenneth
Perle, Richard N., 87

Persian Gulf War (1991), 18, 19, 91–92, 105, 109; analogies to World War II, 99–100; as illustrative of dangers of proliferation, 106–107; rhetoric of, 97–104, 111, 123, 125. *See also* Bush, George; Hussein, Saddam; New world order
Pike, John, 112
Point defense, 9, 79–81, 92, 127. *See also* Strategic Defense Initiative
Population defense, 9, 75–76, 79–81, 92, 123, 127. *See also* Strategic Defense Initiative
Potter, Ralph, 23
Presidential power, 19, 114, 115–116, 118–122, 131
Public debate, 7–9, 19, 39, 114; and technology, 115, 125–131; and U. S. foreign policy, 118–120; implications of SDI for, 115–116, 127–131; insulation of SDI from, 84–90.
Public discourse. *See* Public debate
Public moral argument. *See* Public debate
Public opinion and U. S. foreign policy, 116–117, 120. *See also* Public debate

Quayle, Dan, 99, 102, 112

Rationality, 7, 25, 51, 125–126, 130. *See also* technical reasoning
Reagan, Ronald: administration of, 9, 18; election of, 41; "evil empire" address, 8, 14; March 23, 1983 ("Star Wars") address, 1, 8–9, 17, 65, 66–71, 126; nuclear weapons policies of, 13–14, 45, 54, 61, 66–67; optimism of, 63, 81; reaction to nuclear freeze, 61–64; rhetoric of, 37, 45, 46–48, 65, 93, 106–107, 115, 121, 123–124, 127; "zero option" address, 8

Rhetoric: and history, 21–22; and ideology, 6, 22; defined, 2, 10; of the Cold War, 36–37; pro-war, 5. *See also* Burke, Kenneth; Language; Symbols

Ridenour, Louis, 43

Roosevelt, Franklin Delano, 34–35, 101

Roosevelt, Theodore, 29, 31

Rushing, Janice Hocker, 8, 9, 126

Said, Edward W., 108–110

Saudi Arabia, 97, 100, 106. *See also* Persian Gulf War (1991)

Schell, Jonathan, 15, 53

Schultz, George, 86

Scud missile, 106–107

SDI. *See* Strategic Defense Initiative

Sofaer, Abraham, 85

Soviet Union: acquisition of atomic weapons, 13, 36, 45; as "evil empire," 14, 19, 45, 47, 76, 91, 94, 124; diminishing threat from, 96, 105; fear of, 49, 54, 60–61, 69, 76; nuclear threat from, 13–14, 54, 60–61, 67–68, 93, 95; reforms in, 94–95

Spaeth, Robert, 57–58

Spanish-American War, 29

Star Wars. *See* Strategic Defense Initiative

Steel, Ronald, 31

Stone, Ralph, 34

Strategic Arms Reduction Talks (START), 93, 94

Strategic Defense Initiative: and arms control, 77–78; and deterrence, 79–81; and end of the Cold War, 92–97, 104–113; and innocence, 74, 81–84; and new world order, 91, 104; and nuclear freeze, 75–81, 78; and patriotism, 72; and public debate, 115, 120–122, 127–130; and U. S. destiny, 71–75; announcement of, 1, 65, 66–71; as defensive, 73–74, 93, 122; as point defense, 79–81; as population defense, 75–76, 79–81, 123; as research program only, 66, 73, 84–90; as substitute for disarmament, 11, 17, 18, 19, 62–64; as technological solution to arms race, 8, 18, 83–84, 115; as way to render nuclear weapons obsolete, 68–69, 79, 115, 131; budget problems of, 95–96; first strike implications of, 74–75; future deployment of, 85–86, 93; heroism of, 69–70; objectives of, 6, 78–81; optimism of, 71–73, 81; refocused to GPALS, 107; rhetorical perspective on, 2, 3, 81–84; technical uncertainty of, 84–90, 96, 128. *See also* Global Protection Against Limited Strikes; Reagan, Ronald

Symbols, 4, 9–10, 38, 101, 124; and freedom, 82; and innocence, 81–84; and the pentad, 11–12; as action, 1, 10, 109; as mode of understanding, 2, 6, 21–22, 30, 36, 69; negative implications of, 66, 70, 81–84. *See also* Burke, Kenneth; Language; Rhetoric

Technical reasoning, 7–9, 19, 56; and language, 125–130

Technical sphere. *See* Technical reasoning

Technology, 6, 18, 63, 114; and public debate, 115, 125–130; and U. S. destiny, 71–75, 113, 116; as by-product of language, 10, 18, 38, 82–84; as god-like, 71, 73, 83–84, 129; as new frontier, 19, 39, 63; as solution to arms race, 5, 8, 39, 63–64, 70, 83–84, 91, 104, 126, 128–131; optimism and, 71–73, 107

Teller, Edward, 89

"Third World" nations, 92, 108–110, 113, 131

Tower, John, 92

Transcendence. *See* Burke, Kenneth

Truman, Harry, 13, 37, 42–43, 101, 123

Tsongas, Paul, 87–88

Tuchman, Barbara, 33

Turner, Frederick Jackson, 28

United Nations, 97, 98–99, 103, 104, 109

U. S. foreign policy: and public opinion, 116–118; as discursive, 21, 114, 115, 118, 120–125, 135n.13; as moralistic, 21, 26, 37; dualism in the rhetoric of, 6–7, 36, 98–104, 110–112, 122–125, 130–131; early neutrality in, 26; rhetorical perspective on, 21, 114, 115

U. S. S. R. *See* Soviet Union

Vietnam war, 37, 117–118

Wander, Philip, 6

Washington, George, 26

Weinberger, Caspar, 46, 72, 79, 94, 121

Wilson, Woodrow, 30–34

Wood, Lowell, 89

Woodruff, Roy, 89

World War I, 30–34, 35

World War II, 34–36, 38, 42; analogous to Persian Gulf War, 99–100

Worldview. *See* Burke, Kenneth

X-ray laser, 89